Tales from the

CLEVELAND CAVALIERS

The Rookie Season of LeBron James

Roger Gordon
Foreword by Austin Carr

www.SportsPublishingLLC.com

ISBN: 1-58261-839-9

Publishers: Peter L. Bannon and Joseph J. Bannon Sr.
Senior managing editor: Susan M. Moyer
Acquisitions editor: Dean Reinke
Developmental editor: Mark E. Zulauf
Art director: K. Jeffrey Higgerson
Dust jacket design: Heidi Norsen
Project manager: Kathryn R. Holleman
Imaging: Kerri Baker, Christine Mohrbacher, Heidi Norsen
Photo editor: Erin Linden-Levy
Vice president of sales and marketing: Kevin King
Media and promotions managers: Kelley Brown (regional),
    Randy Fouts (national), Maurey Williamson (print)

Printed in the United States of America

Sports Publishing L.L.C.
804 North Neil Street
Champaign, IL 61820

Phone: 1-877-424-2665
Fax: 217-363-2073
Web site: www.SportsPublishingLLC.com

CONTENTS

FOREWORD

The Cleveland Cavaliers have had about as much fortune as a prizefighter who fractures his forearm in the first round. This franchise has seemingly had more bad luck than any other team.

Who can forget Jim Chones's broken foot in 1976, the troubled times in the early '80s, Michael Jordan's dagger to the heart? There was Brad Daugherty's career-ending back injury and, more recently, Z's infamous foot problems. I, myself, broke a foot my rookie season, then had knee surgery three years later.

But, most of all, it was the Cavaliers' lousy fortune in the NBA Draft Lottery. Finally, though, at long last, we got a break. On the evening of May 22, 2003, the basketball gods looked down and said, "It's Cleveland's turn," by allowing us to win the lottery to gain the rights to select LeBron James with the first pick in the upcoming draft.

You couldn't ask for a better shot in the arm. What happened was like a miracle. The first thing I thought was, "We finally beat the other cities, we finally are starting to head in the right direction."

That night, I was at Champps in nearby Valley View at the Cavaliers' lottery party. It was an emotionally charged evening. There were a lot of people hugging others they didn't even know! Complete strangers! There were some fans who were in tears, just like I was. It meant so much to the area, and the franchise, that it was overwhelming.

I've lived in Cleveland now for more than 30 years, and this is my heart and soul, my livelihood, my whole existence, right here, the Cavaliers. Whatever my role with the team has been, anything that happens to this franchise affects me. And, for something like that to happen, it was a great feeling. We were finally lucky, like so many other teams have been, and used that luck to catapult us to the brink of the playoffs.

A championship is much more attainable now than it was two years ago. Then we had no hope. Now we do. The possibility is definitely there.

—Austin Carr
- Analyst, Cavaliers Television Network
- Director of Community and Business Development, Cleveland Cavaliers
- Guard, Cleveland Cavaliers, 1971-80

PREFACE

When Cleveland Cavaliers fans think of the word "miracle," a remarkable month-long stretch in the spring of 1976 usually comes to mind. That is when the six-year-old Cavs advanced to the Eastern Conference finals and were on the brink of an NBA championship. Included were three heart-pounding, last-second wins over the favored Washington Bullets in the conference semifinals. It came to be known as the "Miracle in Richfield."

What happened on the evening of May 22, 2003, though, might just bump the "Miracle in Richfield" to runner-up. The Cavaliers lucked out, got a break, finally found some fortune. The Cavs had been a laughingstock for much of their lousy past due to poor teams that were the result of inept management (Ted Stepien), bad coaches (Bill Musselman), poor draft picks (David Magley), horrible trades (take your pick from the Stepien ownership era when the team was known as the "Cadavers"), and just plain bad luck (Jim Chones's broken foot that many believe cost the Cavs the '76 NBA Championship).

The Cavaliers wished upon a lucky star, and the heavens shone down on them for once. They won the NBA Draft Lottery, a ping-pong ball drawing held a month prior to the college player draft to determine the draft's pecking order of NBA teams that fail to qualify for the postseason.

The prize for the winning ticket? An 18-year-old kid just out of high school.

LeBron James was his name, reviving the Cavs his game. James was unique. He was the first high school underclassman participating in a team sport to be featured on the cover of *Sports Illustrated* when he was heralded "The Chosen One" as a junior. He led Akron St. Vincent-St. Mary to three state titles. The only year the Irish failed to claim the crown was James's junior year when they were runners-up. He also possessed a maturity level that bewildered everyone.

James brought to the Cavaliers, and the city of Cleveland, instant stardom, instant notoriety. He did not bring immediate success on the court, but he did bring immediate improvement—by leaps and bounds. After an 0-5 start turned to 6-19 a week before Christmas, the Cavaliers, with help from two significant trades in a five-week period, began playing as a team, and found themselves in the thick of the Eastern Conference playoff race.

An injury to point guard Jeff McInnis was a key factor in Cleveland barely missing the postseason. The young Cavs, though, got a taste of what NBA playoff basketball is all about, for the majority of their games down the stretch were do-or-die.

When drafted by Cleveland, LeBron said he'd light up the town like Vegas. He's off to a fine start, and the future does look mighty bright.

ACKNOWLEDGMENTS

I thank Dean Reinke of Sports Publishing, L.L.C., for granting me the opportunity to write this book. Dean stuck his neck out for me, and I am grateful for that. I appreciate the efforts of David Brauer of Sports Publishing in editing the book, Mark Zulauf for his input, and everyone else at SP who contributed.

Also recognized are those who provided their insights, especially Tad Carper and Terry Pluto. Both came through in a big way by also arranging key interviews. Carper supplied valuable information, as well.

I am grateful to those who allowed me access to their P.C.—Mom and Dad, Bruce and Erin, Marianne, and Lee—when mine went haywire as my deadline fast approached. Also appreciated is Marianne's proofreading.

Special thanks to Austin Carr for penning the foreword.

CAVS TIME LINE

MAY 22, 2003
—The Cavaliers win the NBA Draft Lottery, giving them the number-one pick in the draft the next month.

JUNE 26, 2003
—The Cavaliers surprise no one by selecting LeBron James out of nearby Akron St. Vincent-St. Mary High School with the first pick in the NBA Draft.

OCTOBER 29, 2003
—LeBron James scores 25 points, dishes out nine assists, and grabs six rebounds in his NBA debut. James's point total marks the highest ever for a player straight out of high school in his first game in the NBA. The Cavaliers fall, 106-92, to the Kings in Sacramento.

NOVEMBER 5, 2003
—Cleveland makes its home debut before a sellout crowd at Gund Arena. The Cavaliers lose, 93-89, to the Denver Nuggets in the first game at the professional level between LeBron James and Carmelo Anthony.

NOVEMBER 8, 2003
—The Cavaliers win their first game of the season, 111-98 over the Wizards at Gund Arena. LeBron James scores 17 points to go along with eight rebounds and nine assists.

DECEMBER 3, 2003
—Carlos Boozer sets a career high with 21 rebounds in Los Angeles against the Clippers. He also chips in 14 points in a 90-80 loss.

DECEMBER 15, 2003

—The Cavaliers and Boston Celtics complete a six-player trade that sends Ricky Davis, Chris Mihm, Michael Stewart, and a future second-round draft pick to Boston in exchange for Tony Battie, Kedrick Brown, and Eric Williams.

DECEMBER 19, 2003

—Cleveland snaps its 34-game road losing streak with an 88-81 win at Philadelphia. LeBron James sets a then-career high with 36 points. It is the Cavs' first road win since January 12, 2003, at Seattle.

DECEMBER 20, 2003

—Cleveland wins back-to-back road games for the first time since February 18-22, 2002, with a 95-87 win at Chicago. LeBron James scores 32 points and has 10 assists.

DECEMBER 25, 2003

—The Cavaliers make their first appearance on Christmas Day since 1989. LeBron James scores 34 points, while Carlos Boozer adds 18 points and 19 rebounds, but the visiting Cavs fall in overtime to the Orlando Magic, 113-101.

DECEMBER 28, 2003

—LeBron James just misses his first career triple-double with 32 points, 10 rebounds, and nine assists in the Cavaliers' 86-74 win against Portland at Gund Arena.

JANUARY 6, 2004

—Dajuan Wagner makes his first appearance of the season after missing 33 games due to undergoing arthroscopic surgery of his right knee. Wagner plays eight minutes in the Cavaliers' 107-96 win over the visiting New York Knicks.

JANUARY 13, 2004
—The Cavaliers gain their second straight win in Seattle by a 104-96 count. LeBron James posts 27 points, nine rebounds, and nine assists.

JANUARY 17, 2004
—Carlos Boozer scores a career high-tying 32 points, and grabs 18 rebounds, as the Cavaliers rally from a 14-point fourth-quarter deficit to overtake the Utah Jazz and post their first ever win at the Delta Center in Salt Lake City, 102-96 in overtime. LeBron James scores 29 points before spraining his right ankle with 2.3 seconds remaining in regulation.

JANUARY 20, 2004
—Carlos Boozer ties his career high from the game before with a 32-point effort, to go along with 18 rebounds, in the Cavaliers' 99-94 win over the Seattle SuperSonics at Gund Arena. The win marks the first season series sweep of Seattle in franchise history. Boozer hits a career-high 14 of 15 from the line.

JANUARY 21, 2004
—The Cavaliers acquire Jeff McInnis and Ruben Boumtje Boumtje from the Portland Trail Blazers in exchange for Darius Miles.

JANUARY 24, 2004
—Jeff McInnis makes his debut in a Cavaliers uniform and leads the team to a 95-87 win over the Philadelphia 76ers at Gund Arena. McInnis scores nine points and dishes out six assists. The Cavs proceed to win 17 of their next 25 with McInnis in the lineup, including a seven-game winning streak from March 3-16.

JANUARY 28, 2004

—Dajuan Wagner hits a runner with 7.4 seconds left in the game to give the Cavaliers a 94-93 win over the Miami Heat at Gund Arena. Zydrunas Ilgauskas scores a then-season-high 30 points in the win, Cleveland's third straight.

FEBRUARY 1, 2004

—LeBron James sets a career high with 38 points, and Zydrunas Ilgauskas blocks a season-high six shots, at Washington in the Cavaliers' 104-100 win.

FEBRUARY 20, 2004

—The Cavaliers rally from an eight-point deficit with 6:14 remaining in the game to upset the defending NBA champion San Antonio Spurs, 89-87, at Gund Arena. LeBron James scores 32 points and grabs 11 rebounds.

FEBRUARY 22, 2004

—Zydrunas Ilgauskas scores a season-high 31 points and grabs 15 rebounds to help the Cavs knock off the Knicks for the third time in 2003-04, 92-86, at Madison Square Garden. LeBron James scores 22 points in his New York debut.

FEBRUARY 23, 2004

—Jason Kapono scores 13 of his career-high 19 points in the second half as the Cavaliers rally for their biggest comeback win ever. New Orleans leads by 25 with 6:19 left in the second quarter before the Cavs fight back. Carlos Boozer adds 24 points and nine boards.

MARCH 3, 2004

—On LeBron James Bobblehead Night at Gund Arena, James scores a game-high 24 points to lead the Cavaliers past the Atlanta Hawks, 112-80. It would begin a seven-game win streak, the Cavs' longest since they won 10 straight from

November 21-December 11, 1997. That same day, Cleveland waives J.R. Bremer and signs Lee Nailon to a 10-day contract.

MARCH 14, 2004
—LeBron James scores 26 points and Jeff McInnis adds 16 and records 10 assists, as the Cavaliers topple the team with the league's best record, the Indiana Pacers, in a thrilling 107-104 victory at Gund Arena.

MARCH 16, 2004
—The Cavaliers defeat the Chicago Bulls, 111-87, at Gund Arena but suffer a major loss when Jeff McInnis bruises his shoulder and misses eight of the next nine games. It also is the Cavs' last win in their seven-game win streak.

MARCH 27, 2004
—LeBron James sets career highs with 41 points and 13 assists in the Cavaliers' memorable 107-104 triumph over the New Jersey Nets at Gund Arena. Carlos Boozer and Zydrunas Ilgauskas add double-doubles as Cleveland snaps its four-game losing streak. Earlier in the day, the Cavs place Jeff McInnis on the Injured List with a right shoulder bone bruise.

MARCH 29, 2004
—The Cavaliers sign point guard Mateen Cleaves to a 10-day contract. Cleaves, who led Michigan State to an NCAA championship in 2000, plays in four games (two starts) before being released eight days later.

MARCH 30, 2004
—Four Cavaliers score more than 20 points for the first time since April 7, 1997. LeBron James (28), Zydrunas Ilgauskas (26), Carlos Boozer (23), and Lee Nailon (23) combine for 100 points, but it is not enough as the Cavs fall at Dallas, 126-109.

APRIL 6, 2004

—The Cavaliers activate Jeff McInnis and release Mateen Cleaves. McInnis returns to the starting lineup and scores 16 points, plus has 10 assists, but the Cavs fall at home to the Toronto Raptors, 87–86.

APRIL 9, 2004

—The Cavaliers' faint playoff hopes are put to rest as they are outscored, 30–12, in the fourth quarter in a 106–91 loss at Miami.

APRIL 12, 2004

—The Cavaliers close out the home portion of the schedule with a 93–89 win over the Milwaukee Bucks in front of the 16th sellout crowd of the season at Gund Arena. LeBron James leads the charge with 27 points, seven rebounds, and nine assists as the Cavs win for the 23rd time at home on the season—the most since the 1997-98 campaign.

APRIL 14, 2004

—Cleveland ends the season with a 100–90 win at New York against the Knicks. The Cavaliers finish the season with a 35–47 record—the most wins by the team in six seasons. The Cavs finish one game [actually two games with the head-to-head tiebreaker] behind Boston for the eighth and final playoff spot in the Eastern Conference.

Chapter 1

AND THE WINNER IS...CLEVELAND (FOR ONCE)

SOMETIMES YOU NEED TO HIT ROCK BOTTOM

The Cleveland Cavaliers of the mid- to late 1990s were a facsimile of what the National Basketball Association is all about. The NBA covets competitiveness across the board, from L.A. to Boston, Milwaukee to Miami, New Orleans to New York. The league prefers as many teams as feasible to stay in competition for a playoff berth for as long as possible. That is why, for each of the last 21 years, 16 teams have qualified for postseason play. That is more than half of all the teams! Parity is in.

From the 1993-94 season through 1997-98, the Cavaliers won 47, 43, 47, 42, and 47 games—respectable, even admirable, totals—that qualified them for the playoffs in all but one of those seasons. They lost in the first round each time, winning just two games along the way. The Cavs had players talented enough for the team to post decent records, keep the fans coming and qualify for the playoffs, but not nearly good enough to do anything once it got there. It was a vicious cycle.

"In the NBA, generally the rule is you have to get really bad before you get really good," said *Akron Beacon Journal* columnist and author, Terry Pluto. "The problem was, when they moved to the Gund [Arena] (after 24 seasons at the Coliseum in rural Richfield), they didn't want to [get really bad] because they didn't want to lose the fan base. [Former general manager] Wayne Embry was in favor of taking that type of dive, but ownership was not. So they wanted to be decent and hope to get lucky and that sort of thing."

Jim Paxson came aboard as general manager in 1998 and did a formidable job in a tough situation by cutting fat payroll, most notably that of Shawn Kemp, Trajan Langdon, and Andre Miller. And Paxson had enough pull in the organization to do what Embry had wanted to do.

"To Paxson's credit, they didn't know they were going to win the lottery," Pluto said, "but he was willing to take the dive to take a shot at not just LeBron but a Carmelo [Anthony], or just to get a higher pick. It finally got to be so bad after [former head coach] Mike Fratello left, I think they had to get there themselves."

UNTIMELY TRIUMPH

"There's losing, and there's losing with a purpose, and the Cavs lost with a purpose in 2002-03," Bill Livingston, sports columnist for *The Plain Dealer* in Cleveland, said. "It seems like a lot of crust to have asked people to come out to see that sorry product, but it paid off."

It got to the point, though, near the end of the season where fans feared the Cavaliers were going to blow the chance to secure LeBron James by winning too many games. And when they defeated the Toronto Raptors on the final day of the season, it was actually a bittersweet victory. A loss would have left them with a record of 16-66, one game worse than the Denver Nuggets' 17-65 mark. But the victory dropped the Cavaliers into a tie with the Nuggets for the worst record in the league. Consequently, rather than having a 25 percent chance—the highest a team can have—of landing the number one pick, the Cavs had to settle for 22.5 percent odds, the same as Denver.

"I wrote it was a 'must-lose' game," Livingston said, "but of course they won."

"Fans were furious," recalled Bob Karlovec, sports reporter for WKNR-AM 850 in Cleveland.

The next day in *The Plain Dealer* it read, "Cavaliers Win and Lose."

"I think your team is always out there to win," Cavs president Len Komoroski said. "You can never be in a situation where you tell your team not to compete. And in that case, we ended up competing, ended up winning."

THE RIGHT "FIX"

There was a large contingent of fans and media members who were sure that LeBron James would wind up in a large market like New York, Los Angeles, or Chicago since the Knicks, Clippers, and Bulls were in the lottery. The infamous "bent envelope" incident that landed Patrick Ewing in The Big Apple in 1985 was being rehashed, and seemed fresh in everyone's mind.

"People were cursing the lottery," Len Komoroski said, "and also the sense that it was fixed and 'woe is us' because the New York Knicks, the L.A. Clippers, and the Chicago Bulls—teams in the three largest markets in the United States—were in the lottery. And, of course, the sense was that the NBA was going to have it go so one of those teams would win the lottery. As much as you try to explain the integrity of the lottery, there were very few people who were buying that, and they felt it was inevitable that LeBron would end up going to a large market team."

One pessimistic media member was Kenny Roda, sports talk show host on WKNR-AM 850 in Cleveland.

"I remember Kenny had been saying the lottery was fixed and there was no way it was going to work out for Cleveland," recalled Jeff Sack, Metro Networks beat reporter. "I said to him at one point, 'If the lottery was truly fixed, then they would fix it Cleveland's way because, what better way to re-stimulate a market than to bring a hometown hero into it?' Now, I don't believe it's fixed, but if it was, it couldn't have worked out any better."

CROSS YOUR FINGERS

On May 22, 2003, lottery day finally arrived. One ping-pong ball could change the entire identity of the Cleveland Cavaliers. Nervousness, excitement, worry, you name it, pervaded the Cleveland market. *The Plain Dealer* had close to a full-page shot of LeBron James with a Cavaliers uniform superimposed over the top of him with the phrase "Think LeBron" at the top.

"You saw it everywhere in town," Len Komoroski recalled, "and the whole mantra with it was to cut it out, hang it at your water cooler, hang it in your window at your place of business, put it in your cube—wherever you're at—and just keep saying to yourself, 'Think LeBron, think LeBron, think LeBron,' over and over and over again until it becomes reality."

Good fortune had not been a Cavaliers trademark throughout their history, and their luck in the lottery put an exclamation point on it.

"I didn't think they were going to get it," said Bill Livingston. "I told myself, 'Well, [Carmelo] Anthony will be a very nice consolation prize, but it's going to be tough to convince people here because of [LeBron's] local ties and because of the incredible hype.'"

Komoroski put a different spin on it.

"It was interesting because, from a marketplace end, there was a certain sense of, 'Here we have this phenomenal player, arguably one of the greatest high school athletes of all time, right here in our backyard.' And I think there was a pervading sense that, 'Unfortunately, we're only going to get to see him once, maybe twice, a year when he comes in with his visiting team.'"

The media certainly had done a thorough job of dissecting what the possibilities were. It was well known that there had not been a team with the deserving (worst) record that won the lottery since 1990. Ultimately, it did have a bearing.

"I think the market mentality was," Komoroski continued, "'Oh, gee, now we're tied with Denver,' 'Oh my, it hasn't been since '90,' and 'The Shot, The Fumble, The Drive', and everything else being rehashed and relived. We had even lost a coin flip with Denver in the event of a tie that determined what our sequence of balls would be, but it would have impacted us only in a worst-case scenario that would have had Denver at number four and us at number five."

AT THE LOTTERY
New Jersey in New Jersey

Representing the Cavaliers at the actual lottery drawing at the NBA Enterntainment Studios in Secaucus, New Jersey, were team chairman and principal owner Gordon Gund, board member Warren Thaler, and vice president of communications Tad Carper. The Cavs were more than prepared in case "It Happened"—the Cavs won the number-one pick in the draft.

"We had a jersey made up in preparation," Carper said. "It was the first ever LeBron James jersey. We still have it. There were one or two people in the league office who were aware that we had made the jersey, which was in a briefcase I had with me."

When it was announced that the Memphis Grizzlies won the number-two pick, giving Cleveland the top pick, nobody in their wildest dreams could have imagined the caper that Carper would pull next. He dashed on the stage during the commercial break and handed the jersey to Gund.

"Ultimately, everybody was fine with it," Carper recalled. "However, in the heat of the moment, I think it really surprised a lot of people because, after I made the trip on stage, one of the producers of the show (that was broadcast live in prime time on the ABC Television Network) was 'encouraging me' to leave the stage because they were coming back from commercial. When I went back off to the side, a lot of the media was standing there, and I can remember people gasping when we did that, and everybody turned around looking like, 'Who's that guy?'

"One of the media members said, 'Wow, you must've been incredibly confident that you were going to get the number-one pick!' And I said, 'No, we were just incredibly well prepared, just in case.' I mean, it was no secret what we were going to do with that pick and where we were going with it. So, at that point, we felt like, 'Hey, why beat around the bush? Let's go ahead and celebrate.'

"The whole night, I remember carrying around that briefcase, and I must have been the only guy in there walking around carrying his briefcase everywhere he went. I was just thinking, 'Gee, I'm in here and I've got this little surprise in my bag, and if we don't get the number-one pick, nobody will ever know what would've been.'"

Gordon Gund is all smiles as it is announced that the Cavs get the No. 1 draft pick in the lottery on May 22, 2003. (AP/WWP)

Leaving the Past in the Dust

The Cavaliers had gone through some truly tough times in recent years. There were four consecutive seasons of 50 losses or more, including a near 70-loss campaign in 2002-03. Fans were becoming apathetic, which is worse than fans growing angry because, at least when fans are angry, they care. That is why winning the 2003 NBA Lottery was so vital to the future of the franchise. Carper understood the significance.

"As they start going through the announcement, 'Pick number 14, number 13, number 12, 11…as you get closer, the room gets quieter and quieter, and conversation between people from other teams and yourself sort of ceases," he said. "And then you're down to the final two. I felt like a soda can that has been shaken repeatedly for a long period of time, and I knew if we ever got to pop the top on that can, everybody with the franchise was really going to let it out, and I did. I may not originally be from Cleveland, but I still bleed wine and gold.

"Ever since that moment in time, it forever changed the course of the franchise. It's been a whirlwind ever since. Maybe that's because we have gone through some tough times, and now we're headed in the right direction."

The Perfect Storm

Sometimes things just fall into place. Everything comes together. That is what happened with the Cavaliers in the months leading up to the 2003 NBA Lottery.

Said Carper, "The setting was so perfect—Len [Komoroski] likes to use the term 'The Perfect Storm'—because we had switched over to the new logo and colors, Carlos Boozer has that phenomenal year, Zydrunas [Ilgauskas] is healthy and ready to go, so we've got one of the top centers.

"Getting the number-one pick and being able to add LeBron to that equation, it was so right because of the other building blocks that had been placed around it. We were in great shape in terms of the salary cap, we had gone through the tough part and come out the other end, and now it was just so right that it would've been one of the great injustices in sports for that not to happen."

The Lottery of Lotteries

It was the Cavaliers' version of the Super Lotto. However, Cleveland's odds were a whole lot better. The Cavs' 17-65 season in 2002-03 made them legitimate contenders to garner the number-one pick in the 2003 NBA Draft. That is because the NBA utilizes a "lottery" system in which thousands of ping-pong balls are drawn, bingo style. The poorer a team's record, the more ping-pong balls it is awarded and, thus, the greater odds it has of securing a higher pick.

The Cavaliers' luck in the lottery, like with most other facets of the franchise, had been terrible, so fans and media were pessimistic to say the least. It was an exciting time, though, from the day the 2002-03 season ended in April to the Big Night on May 22.

"I was tremendously excited because I had a very good feeling for what this could mean for the marketplace, for the team, and for our employees," Gund said. "We really needed a pickup, and we couldn't have asked for a better one. There are lots of lotteries—and some of them with very big pots—but I don't think any is bigger than that one."

"Behind Bars"

Thaler was one of a handful of individuals sequestered in the actual ping-pong ball drawing room as the lottery was being conducted.

"He was locked up until the show was over," Carper said.

Not even a cell phone signal could get through.

I Can't Drive 55

As Carper was driving to Gund Arena the next morning after flying in to Hopkins Airport, he was so fired up, he had trouble keeping it under 80 mph.

"I was channel surfing the whole way," he said, "and every single station I turned to—even the ones that are music only!—was talking about the lottery. I wanted to get back to work as fast as I could and share in the excitement with everyone there."

I Told You So

Carper and Carlos Boozer used to laugh because their conversations had become stale since all they talked about was the lottery. That's all either one of them wished to talk about. The two of them had just arrived at Gund Arena in Boozer's SUV after a radio engagement at the Cavaliers' flagship station, WTAM.

"Carlos was going to go grab lunch and go back to his apartment," Carper recalled, "so he was dropping me off by the arena. And I was going to leave for the lottery in New Jersey the next morning, so I wasn't going to see him until I got back. I remember him, as I was getting out of his ride, just calmly looking over and saying, 'You know what, Tad, you're gonna get it done, we're gonna get the number-one [pick], I got no doubt,' just as calm and cool as you could imagine. And I said, 'Yep, I'll see you back here in a day!'

Carper ran into Boozer, indeed, the following day, when he got back, in the hallway outside the locker room. Boozer was laughing, with a big grin on his face. 'See, I wasn't worried,' he said. 'I told you we'd get it done.' "

Feeling Like Champps

The Cavaliers' official lottery party was held at Champps in Valley View. Several key people, including clients and friends of the Cavs, were there. It was the epicenter of what was going on in Cleveland, where the marketplace had a chance to engage. Len Komoroski was there, and was hoping upon hope that Cleveland would gain some fortune for once.

"I think, going into the lottery, there was a very much offensive guarded optimism about what could be," he said, "and if you look at it from a Clevelander's perspective, unfortunately our greater athletic moments in certainly the last number of decades have been marked more by near misses, whether it be The Drive, The Fumble, The Shot, or one away from winning the World Series against the Marlins, or whatever the case may be. Unfortunately, I think people were—if you were to ask them in this marketplace—thinking, 'Here's another one to chalk up as a near miss. But the media's there, the place is bustling. They turned a lot of people away hours earlier because that's how full this place was."

Mike Snyder, Cavaliers Radio Network studio host and sports director at WTAM-AM 1100, was there with Austin Carr sorting out all the upper-echelon draft pick possibilities.

"I don't think anybody really even cared, though, about what we had to say about [the Kansas Jayhawks'] Kirk

Hinrich, who was thought to be a high draft pick," Snyder said. "I think we all had some reservations because of the history of the lottery and so forth. Then you couple that with Cleveland sports, and it's like, 'Aw, could we really get this? Could this really happen to Cleveland?'

"I think you kind of prepare yourself to be let down. There was a lot of talk about, 'Boy, even if you're second, you get Carmelo Anthony,' or something like that, so you kind of said that to yourself. But I think, deep down, at least for me, it had to be LeBron, and you were just hoping it would happen. Nothing would make a difference like LeBron, as I think we've all seen. I think everybody knew, especially those of us who'd lived around here, what LeBron James would mean to this franchise. First of all, he is just a phenomenal talent, and he was every bit equal to all of the hype. Number two, he's the local guy, and he's kind of our guy. And the other thing is that there's something with LeBron that he just 'has it.' And I think this franchise needed something like that."

As the sequence kept improving, the excitement in the room expanded right along with it.

"Once they started," Snyder continued, "and began counting down, and they showed, for instance, that the Chicago Bulls were off the board, the place was going crazy. It was like a game where you're in the final seconds."

"It was one of those scenarios of, 'Gee, we're in the top three…and now we're in the top two,' " Komoroski recalled. "In some respects, there's that scenario where, here you are, eye to eye with one of the most exceptional basketball people in the history of the game, both on and off the court, in [Memphis Grizzlies general manager] Jerry West. If there's anyone who has good luck associated with him, it's Jerry West. And here, us, the Cavaliers, we're going toe to toe with Jerry West for that ping-pong ball."

It came down to the Cavs and the Grizzlies, whose deal with the Detroit Pistons that dated back to when they were the Vancouver Grizzlies would give them the number-one pick if they won it. Otherwise, the pick would revert back to the Pistons, and the Grizzlies would drop from a chance at the number-one pick to the end of the line.

"When they announced that Memphis would get the number-two pick, meaning we would get the number-one pick," Komososki said, "it just resulted in an explosion of enthusiasm in our marketplace that would be associated with winning a championship. It was that type of euphoria. Everybody was just crying and hugging and, again, it was as if we had won the championship. It was that type of sense within there."

"When we won it," Snyder added, "you just clenched your fist and said, 'Yes! It's about time!' It was just a Cleveland thing. I just said, 'Yeah! Yeah!' I think I said that several times. 'Yeah! This is right.' That night was a night of raw emotion for everybody. You didn't really think about, 'Okay, what position will he play?' and so forth. You just said, 'We got him! It's about time the sun shone on this town.' It was an exciting day, one in which you remember the shirt you wore, everything about it. For a non-on-the-field/court event, there's nothing I've ever experienced like that in my life in sports."

On Komoroski's drive home that night, all he heard on WTAM was talk about the jinx—the hex—being lifted from Cleveland.

"And the whole question," he said, "being posed then was, 'Now that the jinx is broken, which team will be the first Cleveland team to win a title?' It was imminent that was going to happen since this jinx was broken, especially since it's been since 1964—40 years—going back to the Browns that a Cleveland team has won a championship."

SHINDIG AT SHOOTERS

Sports station WKNR-AM 850 held its lottery party at Shooters in the Flats. Kenny Roda was conducting his drive-time show leading into the lottery when the envelopes were revealed. Roda, along with everyone else, believed Cleveland needed a shot in the arm.

"If it wasn't for bad luck, Cleveland wouldn't have had any luck at all prior to that," he said. "And the way that everybody at Shooters reacted…you had grown men hugging each other, pouring beer over each other's heads as if they had won a world championship.

"To see the second envelope that had Memphis's logo on it, meaning the Cavaliers had won the lottery, I was just thrilled, elated, excited, ecstatic, knowing that finally Cleveland got a break and would have the opportunity not only to get a player of LeBron James's caliber, but a local kid on top of that."

"It was almost as if we knew the Indians were going away and something was taking its place, and that was LeBron," said Greg Brinda, sports talk show host and sports director at WKNR who was also at Shooters that night. "And it was almost like a cult because there was this person there who I hadn't seen. I mean, in the past we've had the Thomes, and the Albert Belles, and the Brian Sipes, but there was really something special that night.

"In just a response to an athlete, it was almost as if they knew that this superstar who was in their backyard was coming to them, and he was theirs. It was pandemonium. You had thought [the Cavaliers] had actually won something. I mean, they did, they won the lottery, but they didn't win any championships, they didn't win any games, they got the right to pick the first player in the draft. It was deafening. It was as big a cheer as I've ever witnessed. It was a wild atmosphere that I hadn't seen since maybe being in a rowdy bar during the baseball playoffs in the '90s."

Bob Karlovec, also at Shooters that night, was in shock. He couldn't believe something good actually happened to the Cavs.

"It was like an 'Oh, my God' kind of moment, like, 'You're kidding.' I didn't think it was going to happen, and maybe that's because I've been around the Cleveland sense of 'Nothing good ever happens to Cleveland in sports' too long. After that, it was, 'This is going to make this team much more interesting to cover now, and basketball's going to be fun in Cleveland again.' And I think a lot of the fans were unbridled in their sheer joy, and that's really what it was, it was just out-and-out sheer joy that finally the graces of sport, the Gods of sport, smiled on Cleveland for a little bit."

It was time—time for Cleveland to get a piece of the pie, time for this blue-collar town that gets no respect to finally get some.

"I said, 'Damn, we've finally got something!" Brinda added. "This is going to be a lot of fun to cover because now the Cavaliers have become something.' Anybody else—even if it was Carmelo Anthony—would have never even approached the importance of this. What it did was, it put the basketball team back on the map because, for three years, it really wasn't on the map. And what made it even bigger was, he was one of our guys, a local guy."

SHOULD WE MAKE AN ALL-NIGHTER OUT OF IT?

The Cavaliers' sales department was more than prepared in case the Cavs won the number-one pick in the draft. The entire staff was at the offices at Gund Arena the night of the lottery.

"We had actually spent hours in the weeks upcoming preparing for, 'Hey, if this happens, how are we going to manage our inventory? How are we going to handle calls that night?'" said Chad Estis, Cavaliers vice president of sales and business development. "Just the whole process of knowing there was going to be an influx of interest."

As Estis and his crew viewed the lottery on television and more and more teams kept getting called, they could feel the excitement starting to build. And when they realized they had it, they celebrated like they had just won a championship.

"We were jumping on each other," Estis recalled, "and it was chaos. And then we all kind of said, 'You know what? I bet these phones are probably ringing. Let's jump out there and see what's going on.' We ran out there and hit the switch on the phones, and they rang consistently from the moment we turned them on until we shut them off at one in the morning. Jim Paxson came down and walked through sales row and was high-fiving everyone. It was just a cool night. The phones would've kept ringing all night had we stayed because there were still some people on hold by the time we got to a point where we just had to cut it off."

At some point, Estis was going to have to call it a night because he knew the next couple of days were going to be vigorous. It would be best, he thought, to get the staff home and get them a few hours of sleep. They returned at seven the next morning and started again. The phones rang steadily for the next three days, through the weekend and into the following week. There were nearly 25 sales people manning the phones, whereas usually there are one or two during the weekend for a few hours.

"And people were buying season tickets!" Estis exclaimed.

Within a week, it was back to normal in terms of the staff becoming aggressive on the phones again. People were much more receptive than in recent years, though.

"We had been pounding sales calls for the years prior to that when the product was struggling," Estis said, "and they would say, 'Hey, I'm not [buying] because of the product.'" He added that fans now were not only buying season tickets, but buying them from as far away as Pennsylvania, Southeast Ohio, and Buffalo. "I mean, it was a complete reverse in how we were received. It was really unbelievable. It was hard for us to imagine.

"It's just such a dramatic difference in how a sales call used to go as compared to how it went after the lottery where people were literally getting on a phone and reading us their credit card numbers, not even paying that much attention to where the seat location was, just so enthused to be in."

THE JAKE ROCKS

Jeff Sack was covering a Cleveland Indians game at Jacobs Field the night of the lottery. He and other media members were sitting in the press box wondering whether the fates would smile on Cleveland for once.

"We were watching the lottery on monitors," Sack recalled. "When the pick was made, you should have seen the reporters in there. We were all like little kids. It may not have rivaled what went on with Austin Carr and the gang with the Cavaliers, but it was a refreshing change of pace for Cleveland, that's for sure. Probably two or three minutes after the pick happened, there was an announcement to the crowd, and the fans went wild. It was pretty funny."

OPPONENTS ON LEBRON

"**H**E IS A COMPLETE BASKETBALL PLAYER ... HE CAN DO THINGS THAT YOU JUST CANNOT TEACH. WHEN I WAS 19 YEARS OLD, I WAS JUST TRYING TO PASS A GEOMETRY CLASS IN COLLEGE."

—*Avery Johnson*, Golden State Warriors

SHALL WE CALL FOR HELP?

David Kelly, sports reporter and talk show host for WTAM, was umpiring a little league game on lottery night. As he was driving home afterwards, he heard the news that the Cavaliers had garnered the number-one pick.

"I think I scared a couple that was driving next to me," he said, "because I started yelling and blowing my horn, and they were looking over at me like, 'What the hell's wrong with that guy?'"

ONCE-IN-A-LIFETIME OPPORTUNITY

When the Cleveland Cavaliers won the number-one pick in the 2003 NBA Draft, many peoples' lives changed, from team management to front office personnel, to the coaching staff, to the players, to the media. The Cavaliers were suddenly in the spotlight. They were no longer a speck on the landscape that is the National Basketball Association.

David Kelly was one of those individuals whose life was impacted by the lottery. He was thrust into the media frenzy that began immediately afterwards. The Cavaliers' fortune did something else for Kelly—it kept him in Cleveland. In the months leading up to the lottery, Kelly was having second thoughts about whether or not he wanted to stay.

"Acquiring LeBron was a feeling that we talk show hosts now were going to have something exciting to talk about from November to April," he explained, "as opposed to past years when that was really a dead time of year with the way the Cavs had played. And, as someone who's ambitious like myself, you start to think, 'Well, how much longer am I going to stay in this market?' This is my home, obviously, but you still want to advance in your field, and I guess I was at a point where I was starting to think, 'Well, should I maybe start to think about leaving Cleveland? Should I maybe start to think about going somewhere else to continue to build my career?'

"And then something like that happens, and you start to think, 'Man, this is going to be an exciting place to be now as far as sports coverage.' Now, it becomes a very vibrant sports community again with just that one element here, so that kind of makes me reconsider my relocation, thinking, 'Hey, maybe I want to stick around in Cleveland and be a part of that.'"

Whereas the arrival of LeBron James kept Kelly put, the heralded megastar from Akron had Rick Noland's wheels spinning in his head. Noland, assistant sports editor for *The Gazette* in Medina County, had two trains of thought heading into the lottery, and they couldn't have been further apart.

"One was, 'They're the Cavaliers, they're going to lose the lottery, that's just the way things have always gone for this franchise,'" Noland said. "And along with that I'm thinking, 'You know, if they do lose it, it's going to take me about five minutes to get over it because my life will be a heck of a lot easier if I don't have to deal with the thousand other people who are going to be in line trying to talk to this kid, interview him, every time he sneezes.'

"But then the opposite extreme of that is, you do this job because you want to be around great players, and you want to be around a team that has a chance to win a championship. And there was nobody out there in the foreseeable future besides him who was going to make that a possibility, and just to be able to cover somebody and be at the center of all that excitement would make all the work seem worth it."

MORE IMPORTANT THINGS THAN BASKETBALL

Jim Paxson was probably the only member of the Cleveland Cavaliers organization for whom the NBA Draft Lottery was not first and foremost on his mind on the day of May 22, 2003. Why, you ask, would the prospect of acquiring LeBron James with the top pick in the upcoming draft NOT be the most important thing on Paxson's mind? After all, he is the Cavaliers' president and general manager of basketball operations.

There was a very good reason that Paxson's thoughts were elsewhere. His wife had just gone through a year of chemotherapy for brain cancer, and the day of the lottery was one of her in-between treatments. The Cavaliers' GM spent all afternoon at the Cleveland Clinic.

"It kind of put things in perspective," he said. "I was nervous about the lottery's outcome during the day, but my focus was on my wife instead."

Paxson and his family were together at home that night, watching the events unfold on television. His hope was to finish in the top three. When Denver came up third, realizing the

Cavaliers actually had a legitimate chance, he was a bundle of nerves and simply wanted to get it over with.

"When they showed the Grizzlies card," he said, "our family room erupted. In one split second, all the things we ended up seeing happen that year kind of flash through your mind, the reality. You do what you have to do, and basically my wife's a lot tougher than I am because of what she had to go through when she went through her treatments.

"The outcome of the lottery, how great it was after the fact, leading into it, those are all very big, but my wife's illness really put it all in perspective—the perspective of life and family, meaning there are a lot more important things than whether we won the lottery or not, at least during that period of my life."

Jim Paxon displays LeBron's new jersey at a news conference at Gund Arena the day after the lottery. (AP/WWP)

Historic to Say the Least

Rick Noland has covered the Cavaliers since 1986 and has witnessed many memorable moments. The evening of May 22, 2003, stands above them all.

"That night was, by far, the biggest night in franchise history," he said. "The only one that would even come remotely close to it would have been the draft night of 1986 when they got [Brad] Daugherty, [Ron] Harper, and [Mark] Price, and they also learned the day before that [John] Hot Rod [Williams] was cleared to play."

Carmelo Would Have Been Just Fine

It was a sure thing, a no-brainer. There was no question in anybody's mind that whichever team won the lottery would make LeBron James the number-one pick in the June draft.

The Cleveland Cavaliers were no different. It was no secret that the floundering franchise was drooling over this phenomenal talent who, two months earlier, had led nearby Akron St. Vincent-St. Mary High School to its third state title in four years. In fact, the Cavaliers probably longed for the services of James more than any other team because of his local ties.

Furthermore, the vast majority of Cavs fans and media members who cover the team believed the lottery would be deemed a failure if Cleveland did NOT win the number-one pick—thus having to settle for any player other than James.

Not Terry Pluto. Although James was his admitted preferred choice, Pluto was just hoping the Cavaliers would pocket the first or second pick.

"Really, I didn't care if it was LeBron or Carmelo," he said. "I knew both were going to be terrific players. I had seen Carmelo play LeBron a couple years before in New Jersey [when Anthony played for Mouth of Wilson (Virginia) Oak Hill Academy], and the last two years he was the only player who was not intimidated by LeBron. I became a huge fan of Carmelo at that point just because I'd seen so many other teams fall apart in front of LeBron at St. V. So I figured he would be, frankly, just about as good as LeBron on the court. He's not as dynamic, but that kid's a good player. LeBron would sell more tickets and bring more hype, but I was just hoping for one of the two. When the number-one pick came up, I was just thrilled."

Chapter 2

LeBron: The Player

Man Among Boys

When you are on the cover of *Sports Illustrated* at 17 years old, you are great at something. For Tracy Austin, it was tennis. For Steve Cauthen, it was horse racing. For LeBron James, it is basketball. James graced the cover of the February 18, 2002, edition of *SI* on which he was billed "The Chosen One" as a member of Akron St. Vincent-St. Mary High School's team. He was the first high school underclassman participating in a team sport to be featured on the magazine's cover. Had James been in the 2002 NBA Draft as a junior, he might have been the number-one pick in that too. He is that good. In high school, he was a man among boys.

"You could see he was the real deal in high school," said Austin Carr. "First of all, physically he was much bigger than everybody else and he was just as quick as these guys at his size. And his understanding of the game was remarkable. LeBron could've averaged 50 points a game in high school if he wanted to but, because of his knowledge of the game and knowing that he couldn't do it by himself, he chose to do it another way. And that showed me a lot of discipline and restraint because, at the high school level, it's all about 'me, me, me,' and LeBron was never that way. When his team needed him, though, he would turn it on. Or if he felt like he just wanted to show somebody that, 'Hey, I'm just as good as you are,' then he would give it to them."

Kenny Roda had been a big supporter of LeBron James since his sophomore year, believing he was big time and could change the course of a franchise.

"I took a lot of flak for hoping the Cavaliers would lose as many games as possible (in '02-03) to have a shot at him," Roda recalled. "That's how good I thought he was."

It is the great unknown whether a gifted player—in high school or college—will continue his prowess in the pros. Some do, some don't. Michael Jordan did. Sam Bowie didn't. Magic Johnson did. Bill Willoughby didn't. James is off to a fine start, but it is still early.

"You never know whether [LeBron's] going to be Kobe Bryant unbelievable," Rick Noland said, "but you could see things then, and he worked, and he always just had that natural charisma that drew people to him, and you could tell he got it. I saw about seven or eight of LeBron's games in high school. The first time I saw him, as a tenth grader, I thought he was unbelievable."

The bigger the stage, the better he did. LeBron was St. Vincent–St. Mary's best player as a freshman in the 1999-2000 season. To some, however, it looked as if he took a back seat to senior Maverick Carter, Ohio's Division III Player of the Year. Keith Dambrot, St. Vincent–St. Mary's head coach at the time, said that was not necessarily the case.

"I don't think he was," said Dambrot, now men's basketball coach at The University of Akron. "LeBron's just such a team player, and always has been, that it may have looked that way."

LeBron James takes to the air for Akron St. Vincent-St. Mary High School against Oak Hill Academy on December 12, 2002. (Reuters/Landov)

"But even then," Noland added, "you could tell he was their best player."

Paul Silas was hired as Cavaliers head coach in June 2003, after the lottery but before the draft, thus Cleveland already owned the first pick. Silas's only chance to see LeBron play after he got the job was when he viewed a tape of the McDonald's All-American game (played some two months prior).

"It was difficult to assess him at that point," Silas said, "because he was just so much better than those kids. He wasn't making a lot of outside shots but, as far as the rest of his game—the quickness, the penetration to the hoop, the passing, the understanding of how to play the game—I thought that was superb."

THE REAL DEAL

From his first game as a professional when he shocked the basketball world with a remarkable performance against a very good Kings team in Sacramento, the 6-foot-8, 240-pound LeBron James proved time and again that four years of college ball would have done nothing but delay his NBA fame and fortune. He was ready for the pros—more than ready.

"The magnitude of all the hoopla surrounding LeBron was the most shocking thing to me," said Paul Silas. "It was just overwhelming, mind-boggling. I had never witnessed anything like it, especially a kid who has never played a pro game, and here he was, getting endorsements, and people were calling him the next Michael Jordan, and all those kind of things."

Silas preferred to take the approach of "Hey, let's wait and see, we're trying to put too much on this kid, just let him ease in.

"But that was not going to happen," he went on. "The expectations were just too much and, to my surprise, he didn't disappoint."

"I didn't know much about LeBron," said Joe Tait, Cavs radio play-by-play announcer and vice president of broadcasting. "I knew he was a heck of a high school talent, but I've seen high school kids come into the pros before and lay large eggs, although I did think he was better than most of them. I don't think anybody had any clue as to how good he was eventually going to be, and I don't think he's even scratched the surface. The kid has got some real tools."

Bruce Drennan thought the Cavaliers would be improved just by the nature of LeBron's presence, but not to the extent that they were.

"I figured he'd be a fast learner. I knew he would be the draw that he was on the road attendance-wise," said the WKNR-AM 850 sports talk show host, "but I didn't think he would make the major impact that he did on the league playing-wise in his rookie season. That was astonishing considering he spent half the year as an 18-year-old and the rest of the season as a 19-year-old. It's mind-boggling."

Drennan added that it is disturbing to him when he hears criticism of James for his outside shooting.

"You watch," he said, "you give him two to three years, he's going to develop into a great outside shooter. He's one of these special players who we should be grateful that we are able to see in his infancy, and see the team grow with him. He's so gifted, and his court awareness and passing are what I love the most about him. He's so unselfish."

Silas concurred.

"Once his shooting, and defense, too, improve," he said, "he has the size, strength, and intelligence to go on to a Hall of Fame career."

ON THE ROAD TO GREATNESS MODE

LeBron James has the skills, size, strength, savvy, and smarts to attain greatness. Barring injury, he has got what it takes to be considered one of the finest players of all time when it is all said and done.

"In my day," Bill Livingston said, "we talked about Jerry West and Oscar Robertson when I was a young guy following basketball. Then I was privileged to cover the Dr. J teams for six years in Philadelphia, and saw Magic and Jordan and Bird. LeBron James wants to be on that list of players, and right now he seems willing to spend the time on his game that would enable him to become a viable player there. Other than injury or self-satisfaction like what claimed [former Cavaliers center] Shawn Kemp, I think this guy's motivation to succeed is so high that he wants to be on the short list of great players ever, and he has made a wonderful start toward it."

James began "getting it" the latter part of the year when he started seeing the light on defense, getting over screens, setting his man up, being more tenacious, and rebounding when needed.

"He really didn't have to do those things [in high school]," Paul Silas said. "If he continues to improve each year as much as he did last year, there's no doubt in my mind the only thing that could hold him back would be getting injured. When *he's* not very good, *we're* not very good."

"Once he's settled in and understands the league, and he's comfortable with the referees and with the traveling and all of that," said Austin Carr, "LeBron has the potential to be a triple-double threat every night like Jason Kidd. But 20 [points], five [rebounds], and five [assists] is phenomenal for a kid coming out of high school. If he works on his individual defense and takes that as more of a challenge like [Michael] Jordan did, he'll reach that next level. He knows he has to work on his outside shot, too. Once he develops that, he will round off his game, and then there's no telling how far he can go."

James has the uncanny knack of seeing the action in slow motion, or being one play or pass ahead of the others.

"I can only compare it to a young Larry Bird or a young Magic Johnson," said Jeff Sack, "and the passing ability certainly would be up there with a young Magic and a young Isiah Thomas. Those are things that are innate, they can't be taught."

Kenny Roda concurred.

"The only guys who have that are Magic, Lemieux, Gretzky, Jordan, Bird…The Chosen Ones," he said.

RECORD ROOKIE

LeBron James in 2003-04 became the first Cavalier in franchise history, and youngest player ever, to be named the NBA Rookie of the Year. James, who averaged 20.9 points per game, 5.5 rebounds, and 5.9 assists, received 78 out of a possible 118 first-place votes. He was also voted the Eastern Conference Rookie of the Month each month during the season. He and Denver's Carmelo Anthony, who finished second in the Rookie of the Year voting, became just the third and fourth rookies in NBA history to receive Rookie of the Month honors every month of their rookie seasons (Anthony achieved the feat in the Western Conference).

LeBron James skies his way to another dunk. (AP/WWP)

"If you compare LeBron right now with the best players in the NBA," said Rick Noland, "I'm not sure he'd be in the top 10, but if you put age and potential improvement into that equation, I think he'd be in the top three or four."

According to *Akron Beacon Journal* sports editor Larry Pantages, Cavaliers fans are witnessing a superstar athlete of monumental proportions who comes along about as often as snow flurries on the Fourth of July.

"We're blessed," Pantages said. "This kid, to me...the sky's the limit, and it looks like he can be here for a while, and Cleveland can be in the same breath with the Lakers."

HE KNOWS WHEN TO LEAD

Statistics are important to LeBron James. However, the kind of stats that are vital to him are those of wins and losses, not individual points, rebounds, and assists. James is the ultimate team player.

"I think LeBron was almost too unselfish when he first started with the team," said Jeff Sack. "And that goes back to the fact that he came into media day and said, 'This is not my team. When I first went to SV-SM, I was a freshman, and I had to pay my dues, and I had to earn my role as a leader there. And I'm going to be doing the exact same thing here with the Cavaliers. This is Ricky's team, this is Z's team.' And I think he was reticent to take a leadership role as long as Ricky Davis was with the team."

LeBron was taking a back seat.

"Would the team have won another four or five games if LeBron hadn't shown that deference and respect? Possibly," Sack continued. "But, again, in LeBron's way of doing things, and LeBron's way of growing up, and LeBron's history of athletics, and LeBron's history of being in organized sports, this is the way things are done. So he was just following the rules of order as it were."

Once the disgruntled Davis was shipped to Boston early in the season, the last restraint on James as a basketball player was shed. At that point, he began to exert more leadership and willingness to take over down the stretch—possibly a little too much.

"He made a couple of decisions to try to win a game," Sack opined, "that may have not been the smartest in the world, ones that, had he handed off to somebody else, they may have had a better shot. But because he had become such a leader, he felt it was his job to either make it or break it."

UNEXPECTED SURPRISE

Most NBA pundits predicted LeBron James would average anywhere from 10-15 points per game. Bill Livingston was no exception. Like everyone else, he was overwhelmed with the rookie's offensive output.

"When I was asked on Les Levine's television show before the season to come up with a good year for LeBron," Livingston said, "I said 12-15 [points per game] and 40 percent shooting. Well, the 40 percent shooting was pretty accurate. He was slightly better than that. But he averaged 20.9 points, he was in the top 15 in the league. No one could have expected that."

Outdoes the Doctor

When Julius Erving—a.k.a. Dr. J—arrived on the NBA scene in the fall of 1976 as a Philadelphia 76er following five seasons in the American Basketball Association, it was a real event.

"I covered Julius Erving," Bill Livingston recalled, "and he had the enormous pressure of basically representing the ABA (from which four teams merged into the NBA). People were saying, 'Could these guys play?' And it was not as much pressure by any means as LeBron James put up with, because it wasn't 24/7 cable news, the Internet, and all of that then. And LeBron exceeded the hype, which is amazing. I told Gordon Gund that the most exciting thing in my years around the league, and that goes back to 1973-74, had been covering Julius Erving's debut in the NBA—until now."

Just Routine

LeBron James could typically be counted on for at least one spectacular play per game. That is a product of James's marvelous talent and the nature of the game he plays.

"Football is so dependent on the spear-carriers and the offensive line," Bill Livingston explained, "and in baseball you can go out there and maybe [Omar] Vizquel only gets routine ground balls that day and doesn't have a chance to make any kind of play. The beauty of basketball is you get so many more chances to show athletic ability, and almost every game LeBron gave you a 'WOW' play."

LeBron James slams one home. (Jeff Zelevansky/Icon SMI)

Prodigy

"Prodigy," according to *Webster's Third New International Dictionary*: "Something out of the usual course of nature…something extraordinary or inexplicable…one that excites admiration or wonder. …"

There are prodigies in the science field, in mathematics, economics, the arts…sports, too. LeBron James just might be one on the basketball court.

"LeBron has an acute basketball awareness," Greg Brinda said, "that is something special. Combined with his physical lottery that he won by his parents mating and giving him the physical qualities, he's combined that with an incredible knowledge and feel for the game of basketball. He really has it all. It's kind of almost freakish to watch somebody who is so young but is still a complete player. LeBron certainly has things to learn, but he understands the game better than a lot of people, including some guys who have been in the league for four or five years.

"When the team started 0-5, I thought to myself, 'This is a good young player on a really bad basketball team.' You could see that he could play. I mean, we didn't really know how well he could play. It was pretty early into his professional career, yet you could see that he had basketball instincts to play at any level, even at a young age at that level. You could see that right off the bat. We didn't really know how consistent he would be all year, and he proved to be very consistent. He blew away my expectations. By just watching him play, I was astounded."

Former Cavaliers assistant coach Mark Osowski, who passed away unexpectedly some four months after the season ended, echoed Brinda's sentiments and then some.

"LeBron's a smart person," Osowski said, "and he has a high basketball IQ."

A+ ATTITUDE

LeBron James is without a doubt the Cavaliers' best player. He is a tremendous talent. What makes him extra special, though, is the fact that he is a team player and is coachable, too. With all of the "me-first," stats-starved prima donna players these days, James is a refreshing change of pace.

"LeBron is a great, young basketball player with such a bright future," Mark Osowski said. "He is very dedicated about the game of basketball. He worked on his game to try to put himself and his team in a position to succeed. He's a team-first guy, and what's important to him is to win. That's part of what makes him such a great teammate. He's just a great, great guy to be around on and off the floor. He's going to do whatever he can to be the best player that he's capable of, to help every team that he's with have success."

RESPECTS THE GAME

If the names "Bob Cousy," "Oscar Robertson," and "Walt Frazier" were dropped among a gathering of today's NBA players, many of them would have a difficult time deciphering who they are. LeBron James would have no problem identifying the men as three of the greatest players ever to don an NBA uniform. All three are in the Hall of Fame.

"LeBron knows the history of the NBA," said Mark Osowski, "and he knows the teams that have won and had success. He respects the game of basketball, he's aware of the players who came before him who paved the way."

Threes Are Wild

As sensational a season as LeBron James had his rookie year, there still are facets of his game he must improve on, one being his outside shot, which was cited as a weakness. And LeBron is known for using criticism as a motivational tool.

"It did amuse me at times when LeBron would say, 'Keep writing that I can't shoot, it's inspirational,'" recalled Bill Livingston. "Well, as long as you're going to shoot 29 percent from the arc, you're damn right I'm going to keep writing that you can't shoot. That was a general address to skeptics heard time and time again."

Rookie Wall? What Rookie Wall?

Like any rookie, LeBron James struggled at times, was not up to par. But unlike most rookies, he always bounced back—instantly.

Opponents on LeBron

"Go beyond the individual, the guy has it. He has it. He's got poise, he's got presence, he's got vision. He's got command of his game. He's one of those guys who's just an intelligent basketball player, on top of being a superior talent. So, what do you have? You've got greatness."

—*Jeff Van Gundy*, Houston Rockets head coach

"He never really hit that kind of 'rookie wall' that people talk about," Jim Paxson said. "During exhibition season, he looked like he was searching—for instance, 'When do you take shots?'—and looking back on it, I think he was just surveying the landscape to figure out what he needed to do when the opening bell rang to kind of go forward."

Teams adjusted along the way, but so did James.

"And that's where I think his gift is his overall intelligence for the game," Paxson added, "and having said that, I still think he's going to continue to get better and grow as a player because he's only 19."

BACK TO BASICS

Even a player of LeBron James's stature has certain areas of his game that call for improvement. In James's case, most would agree his shooting and defense are the culprits.

"He needs to become not just a better shooter," Jim Paxson said, "but needs to improve his shot selection at times. He needs to get to the basket more so he can get to the foul line more."

James shot just under 42 percent from the field. That needs to escalate.

"He'd take a lot of perimeter shots," said Paxson, "but anybody who takes a lot of perimeter shots isn't going to shoot a high percentage. I think LeBron should be, as he gets better, a 45-46 percent shooter because he'll take better shots, and he'll get to the basket more because he's got good form. From watching him in high school and coming in, I was never concerned that he wouldn't be an adequate shooter from the perimeter. I always thought that wasn't going to be a huge hurdle for him because he worked on his game."

Defensively, James must concentrate and not become side-tracked. He needs to focus on the task at hand.

"LeBron really is a floater and a chaser and plays the passing lanes. He got lit up by quite a few guys," Rick Noland said. "If he wants to play [defense], he's going to stop the guy, but he tends to turn his head a few times and chase the ball rather than see the ball, and his man. He tries to make the steal and the run-out dunk. Sometimes, he forgets to go to the defensive boards because he's leaking out looking for an outlet pass on the break."

In high school, James was able to overcome a lack of fundamentals with sheer athleticism. He could get away with it then.

"He'd just block shots at the rim at the last minute," Noland continued. "He definitely likes to get out and get the crowd excited and get everybody into the game. But that's not to say he's not a great fundamental player, because he is. He's 19, though. He's one year out of high school, so if that's the biggest thing anybody can find wrong with him, then he's going to be a pretty darn good player."

WELL-ADJUSTED

Every rookie, and every young player, who comes through the NBA must acclimate himself to the league. And according to Mark Osowski, LeBron James did a fine job of that.

"He was able to learn about the other players," Osowski said, "and learn about the referees and their role in the game. He adjusted quite well, and it seemed that the refs had respect for LeBron even though he is a young player."

LeBron James brings the ball up the court. (EPA/Landov)

I Tried, Coach

Point guard was not LeBron James's position in high school. But when Paul Silas asked him to play the point out of desperation early in the season, he gave it his best shot.

"It was just a little bit too much for him," Silas said. "I saw that early on, but I had nowhere else to turn, so I think he handled it about as well as anyone could have. Everything I asked him to do, he tried it."

Thank You, God

LeBron James is not your typical 19-year-old. His prowess on the basketball court proves it. James also does not possess your ordinary 19-year-old body. His astounding strength affirms it.

"He's 19, and the kid's stronger than most people who are 25, 26," Cavs forward Ira Newble said. "I'm impressed because it's natural strength. I mean, he didn't have a chance to lift that much coming from high school to the NBA. God gave him a gift—the right body for the league. His one-leg takeoff was so strong that he would finish in a crowd and still dunk the ball with ease, with people grabbing on and trying to foul him."

C'mon, Ref

One particular referee seemed to treat LeBron James a little tougher than most refs did. Apparently, this particular referee believed James needed to pay his dues and earn his stripes.

"I don't know if this referee was trying to teach him a lesson or just had an ego trip," Ira Newble said. "He would make comments like, 'You better tell young fella to quit crying. He's too young, he hasn't earned those calls yet.' Even though they might've been fouls, he didn't want to call them and give him the respect. And LeBron really let it be known—well, at least he let it be known to me on the court—that this ref was making it difficult for him on purpose. LeBron would just look at him like, 'Yeah, all right.'"

Chapter 3

LeBron:
The Person

He Just Has "It"

The unique thing about LeBron James is that he is not only a great basketball player but a fine individual, too. He embodies a maturity level rarely found in a veteran, let alone a teenaged, NBA player. He seems to know what to say and when to say it. He handles the onslaught of media—from around the world, no less—with remarkable grace.

The media wave began in high school and it prepared him well. St. Vincent-St. Mary played its home games at the nearby University of Akron's James A. Rhodes Arena, a much larger venue than the SV-SM gymnasium, for most of James's last three years to accommodate the demand for tickets. James and his teammates embarked on a nationwide tour his senior year in which they competed against the finest high school teams in the nation. They played in front of sold-out crowds in big-time venues such as UCLA's Pauley Pavilion and Gund Arena, and even played live on ESPN twice! Thus, by the time James arrived in the NBA, the glare of the spotlight was old hat.

"He was used to it," said Rick Noland. "It wasn't any different for him as a number-one pick in the NBA than it was as a 16-year-old kid in high school. He's smart enough to know that he's a corporate spokesman for a lot of companies. He needs to have positive publicity, but it just seems to come so natural to him."

"LeBron didn't make any missteps," said Bill Livingston. "He didn't say a thing wrong. [Denver Nuggets rookie] Carmelo Anthony did, when he pouted and refused to enter a game because he was upset that his teammates thought he was

LeBron James and Carmelo Anthony concentrate on the game at hand. (Icon SMI)

shooting too much. That cost him some, I think, in the Rookie of the Year voting even though he apologized the next day. I was very impressed by LeBron's maturity. There was nothing in his past to indicate that he would handle it this well.

"Everything about him shouts an entitlement guy. Fawned on from the eighth grade on, he basically was too 'dirty' to go to college. He was just one of those kids you can't recruit because he had taken so much stuff that's in violation of amateurism rules. The Hummer incident was just rubbing the kind of 'horse and buggy' Ohio High School Athletic Association's nose in it. He did not have the most stable home environment, either. And yet, the way he just kind of stepped out of that background and carried himself like this really does kind of convince you that there are some people who are just born to play this game."

How could a kid right from high school possibly be good enough to be a top player in the NBA? How could he justify a hundred-million-dollar endorsement contract—Tiger Woods money—before he ever played? And he did it all.

"It's absolutely remarkable," Livingston said.

"Instead of 19 years old, you'd think he's 29 years old," said Bruce Drennan. "I've never seen anything like it in my career, anybody this young, this good, this national awe about him, the fact that he's received so much attention. Being under the spotlight like that, to handle himself in the fashion that he does is truly incredible."

Added Greg Brinda, "I don't think anybody at that age, considering the hype, the pressure, the money, could have ever done a better job than LeBron."

James has a modesty about him that endears him to everyone around him.

"The thing that you really enjoy about LeBron," Paul Silas said, "is that he talks about winning. He'll be the first one to admit that he makes a mistake, and it just carries over. That's the most important thing, that's what makes it all work. I think that's what draws him to people and what draws people to him. He has the capacity to kind of mesmerize because he is so intelligent, and understands, and says the right things. He just has a sense of what to do at the right place at the right time, and that's God-given. He's very approachable and has a humility about him, and that's just who he is. It's not phony.

"I would assume, along the line somewhere, someone had to talk to LeBron about having the right attitude, that kind of thing. Who, I don't know. But they did, and he took it to heart."

Austin Carr echoed the coach's sentiments. He called James a "thoroughbred" in the business—a guy who understands what's going on around him.

"The way I look at it," Carr said, "he was born with it. Granted, he has good people around him, and there are a lot of things said about his mother's past, but she had to do something positive with him, and the Walker family did a lot for him. They actually raised LeBron for a while when his mother was having her problems. But he just has a good understanding of common sense and what to do and what not to do.

"His body is God-given, too. Naturally his football background helped him develop a lot of that. But hell, I played

LeBron Gets Hit

(Over and Over)

LeBron James had the most popular page on NBA.com during the 2003-04 season, with more than 3.1 million views, ranking ahead of the likes of Allen Iverson, Yao Ming, Kobe Bryant, and Carmelo Anthony.

with guys his size in high school, the same size as him. My center was 6-10, 250, a black belt in karate. One forward was 6-7, 220, the other forward was 6-5, 210, and I was 6-2, 190. LeBron was larger than everybody else, but it's not like there aren't any other guys his size. He has a special gift of talent mixed with knowledge that most kids his age didn't, and don't, have.

"LeBron has star power, so he brought that with him. Because of the way he handles himself, he does not offend people, he stays pretty humble, and people gravitate to that. The only problem I had in my mind was whether he'd be able to deal with the hoopla, and live up to it, because they almost put him on a pedestal that you would think nobody could reach. But LeBron handled all of that. I'd give him an 'A.'"

According to Terry Pluto, 90 percent of becoming a professional athlete is genetic. Attitude, he said, is what separates the best athletes from the rest of the pack.

"LeBron had pretty close to a B average all the way through St.V.," Pluto said. "And people will tell you, and he will say, it's not because he studied day and night, he's just smart. So that helps, and he's able to see and understand things.

"It's kind of like if God were to sit down and say, 'What body would be good for a basketball player?' This would be it: 6-7, 242 pounds, and seven percent body fat. And not only that, He put kind of a Michael Jordan-type brain in it that understands it: 'You've got to play within a team concept, and you've got to at least give your coaches some sort of respect. You have to go through token interviews, you'd represent something more than just it all being about you.' Some guys need 10 years to learn that, but some guys figure it out in about 10 days."

Those who have watched the development of LeBron aren't surprised by how he has stayed so humble. Whereas many professional athletes become conceited and self-centered because of the huge amounts of money that are thrown their way, James is not like that.

"LeBron actually just wants to fit in and contribute, basically give his heart to win. It's completely genuine," Ira Newble said. "Unfortunately, the opposite happens to a lot of guys, whether it's the organization, the coach, or the media that puts them in that position. LeBron didn't really want any part of that, because he didn't want there to be any separation [within the team], and he wanted everybody to kind of be one as a team and do it together. We wouldn't have done as well as we did had LeBron not had that attitude. When you have guys who are arrogant and big-headed or what have you, other guys on the team might take offense to that, and you start having underlying problems that distract the team and create too much separation, and you can't really focus on everybody being together."

LeBron even impressed Gordon Gund.

"The times I've talked with LeBron privately," Gund said, "you get the sense of this young man who's got this very, very unique talent on the court, and an equally unique talent off the court in terms of the way he sees things. He's not complex, he's very simple, he's very team-oriented, he is dedicated and determined, and confident that he will be the best in the game during his time playing. And yet, when he's talking to you, and he stretches that long body out like a 19-year-old and sort of leans back in the couch, you see the contrasts of the youth and this uncanny maturity off the court and, of course, knowing of that ability on the court. It's quite a combination."

What about burdens off the hardwood?

"All the family pressures, and friend pressures, and sordid cousin pressures, and everything else that comes from playing at home ... I wondered how that would play out, if that would cause problems," Terry Pluto said. "And it was just the opposite. LeBron handled everything with such grace, it was like he was 32 years old and had been in the NBA for 10 years."

There are always going to be temptations, however, especially for a star the magnitude of LeBron. That is only to be expected.

"And there's probably going to be something that comes up that's not going to reflect well on him," added Pluto, "just because he's human. But what he did was remarkable."

James's good nature even turned an 83-year-old woman into a Cavs fan. Ruth Mary Tscholl of Canton, Ohio, has always been a basketball fan because she has grandchildren who play. She never really was interested in the Cavaliers until she began following LeBron. In fact, she was not even aware of James before he came to the Cavs.

"I was fascinated by the way he handled himself," said Tscholl, who remains active as co-owner of a local resale clothing store and an avid golfer. "He must have had the mentality that accepted the teaching he had through the people he had in his life from 12 years old through high school. I think he had very, very good guidance by people who happened to come into his life. I feel that he certainly didn't have much of a home life. I think his teachers had very, very good family values. He evidently adopted things well.

"I read that, at the age of 11, everybody wants to be a hero, but coaches and mentors try to tell them, 'This is not how you win at sports, this is not how you do it. It's a team game, and you play as a team.' And LeBron listened to what they said, and he was capable of a lot more because of that. I'm sure some of it is innate.

"I think LeBron brought something to our locality, and to the game, that's been very worthwhile. I respect him because of his attitude, and because I think athletes are so looked up to, and I think it's great to have somebody looked up to who can have as much respect as he does. I think that's very, very important, because it has a big influence on our young generation. You never hear anything bad about him in the news. He's a role model for lots of young people. He certainly has

LeBron James. (Jon Adams/Icon SMI)

added to my fun of watching the team. I live alone, and it makes coming home fun."

SOUND SUPPORT SYSTEM

LeBron James's mother, Gloria, has been criticized or, rather, "roasted over the coals," throughout the years for how she has conducted herself, especially when LeBron was in high school. She certainly wasn't reluctant to revel in her son's prosperity. Many felt she was boasting.

"Gloria was definitely guilty of over-exuberance," said Jeff Sack, "but that's pride coming through. Is it the classiest way, is it the most accepted way in today's P.C. society? Probably not. Can I see her possibly being the butt of jokes because of that type of behavior? Yes. But hey, at least she was involved, at least she was there. I've heard other people talk about the fact that she wasn't really involved in LeBron's academic or athlet–

OPPONENTS ON LEBRON

"WITH EVERYTHING THAT'S GOING ON IN HIS LIFE, NOT TOO MANY 19-YEAR-OLD GUYS WOULD BE ABLE TO HANDLE THAT WHOLE THING. THAT'S A CREDIT TO HIS PARENTS, HIS MOTHER, HIS HIGH SCHOOL COACH, HIS MENTOR, WHOEVER KEPT A CLOSE EYE ON HIM GROWING UP. THEY OUGHT TO FEEL PROUD OF THEMSELVES."

—*Aaron McKie*, Philadelphia 76ers

ic careers until the eighth and ninth grades but again, there are a lot of folks out there, there are a lot of parents out there, who wouldn't have become involved even at that point.

"For all the ribbing and ripping this woman has taken, I give her all the credit in the world. I mean, this is a woman who had a child at 16 years old, certainly did not live the easiest of lives. I mean, they grew up in Section 8 housing. Yet this was her most important job in life, raising this young man, and she did a heck of a job."

In addition to his career as a beat reporter for Metro Networks, Sack is also director of education at the Ohio Center for Broadcasting. He enjoys integrating his two professions and shared his thoughts.

"I talk to my students all the time," he said, "and one of the first things I ask the class when school commences is, 'Where do the best basketball players in the world play?' And, invariably, what they'll say to me is the NBA, and I'll shake my head, 'No.' And then they'll start talking about the Olympics and, again, the answer is no. And then they'll start talking about specific college programs, and the answer is no.

"And then one person will finally get it, and they'll say the playgrounds, and I'll say, 'Expand on that.' They'll say, 'Rockport, Massachusetts.' I'll say, 'Okay.' They'll say, 'Watts, California.' I'll say, 'Okay.' They'll say, 'Gary, Indiana.' I'll say, 'Okay.' And then I'll say, 'Okay, you're right on that. Now, why aren't these guys playing in the NBA? These guys can make cross-court passes that will take your breath away, and make slam dunks that will make most NBA players look like they're playing in a CYO league. But they're playing on street courts with sometimes no nets, in front of crowds of tens, not thousands. And why aren't they playing in the NBA?' And the answer is because although they can play the game of basketball, they can't play the game of life. Gloria taught LeBron how to play the game of life. Whether this was due to her tutelage, or the example she set, or it was innate, who knows? But this young man is definitely on a mission."

James has had so many individuals involved in his life, it would be tempting for an outsider to say, "My God, he has this big posse!" But the fact is, he has had different families, different people, who have actually helped him along the way, and it is not like these are people who have just arrived now that he is a success and has millions of dollars.

"They've been with him from the days when he didn't have a nickel," said Mike Snyder. "And I think it's worked out better maybe than he thought, to be able to have them around and be able to see him play, where you thought maybe sometimes playing at home would've just brought those extra pressures. And he seemed very sincere about how he's enjoyed having that, and the fact that, for people who he's grown up with and who have been part of his life, it's been easy for them to go see him play."

All this success is not without its drawbacks. Of course, there are the ever-present golddiggers lurking of whom LeBron must be wary.

"There are probably a whole bunch of vultures out there taking aim at him," Ira Newble said, "because, in their minds, they know he's young, and they think they can play with his mind and get him. But he's got a lot of good people around him who help him stay focused, so he doesn't get caught up in that too much."

Media Friendly

Dealing with the media barrage upon his arrival in the NBA was not a big deal to LeBron James. Having survived the media hailstorm that was thrust upon him in high school, it was no wonder.

"Covering LeBron has been unbelievably easy," said Rick Noland, adding James is quite accommodating, more so even than many veteran players. "He can turn it on when he has to. He's charming, he understands that the media has a job to do, and why fight it? If he sets 10 minutes aside a day, he can deal with everybody in those 10 minutes all at once. It's not like we all sit down and have one-on-one, 30-minute interviews. You just stand in a line 10 deep. He answers every question, and he does it politely, and he really does seem to be enjoying it. It's not like it's a daily chore for him. He's been great in that area. He's fun to listen to."

James is a master at granting media requests and, at the same time, keeping his teammates from turning on him. They have no qualms about the spotlight shining on the superstar.

"He just blends those two perfectly," Noland said. "And his teammates know that he's the reason why there are 20,000

LeBron James conducts one of his many media sessions. (AP/WWP)

people in the stands and 50 media people at their games, because almost all of those guys were there the year before when there were 5,000 fans and 10 media people there. So what's good for him is good for them."

The young star was so concerned about disruptions in the locker room with the media volume, sometimes he would conduct his postgame sessions outside in the hallway.

"Depending on where we were," said Tad Carper, "he would come out because you just can't have that mess in your locker room," noting that Madison Square Garden and The Palace of Auburn Hills, for instance, have notoriously small dressing areas.

Kid Connection

Perhaps it is because he remembers what it was like being a youngster in awe of a superstar athlete. Maybe it is because he still is a kid in some respects. For whatever reason, LeBron James holds a special place in his heart for his young fans.

For example, at the first media session of the NBA Summer League in Boston, James trudged quite a distance to the interview room through throngs of fans, for the venue was an old college gymnasium not built for that purpose. After the session ended, he had to pass through a semi-public area to return to the locker room.

"We got past the ropes where a lot of the autograph seekers were standing," recalled Tad Carper, who was with him. "We were past them, and LeBron heard some little kid calling out his name. He stoped, turned around, went back, and specifically signed a couple of kids' autographs, and then turned around, and we continued on back to the locker room."

LeBron James has a lot to be happy about. (Jeff Zelevansky/Icon SMI)

Happy Cav

There were rumblings prior to the 2003 NBA Draft Lottery that LeBron James did not care to play for the Cavaliers. After all, the Cavs were coming off a season in which they lost nearly 70 games. James, though, proved those rumors false from the day the Cavs won the lottery.

"I had a chance to sit with LeBron after he was named Rookie of the Year, and he kind of opened up to me," Mike Snyder recalled. "It was probably the best interview that I've done with him in terms of where he was just relaxed and we were kind of away from the spotlight for a little bit. When I asked him about playing at home and about how he's handled it, what really made me feel good—and I think for Cavaliers fans, especially—is that he said it's worked out well for him, that this just couldn't have worked out better."

Chapter 4

THE KING'S COURT

CARLOS BOOZER
Lunch Box Mentality

One man cannot do it alone. Michael Jordan is proof positive.

Of all the team sports, though, basketball is the one in which two men, maybe, can. Win a championship, that is. Thus, as talented as LeBron James is, he does need help. One Cavalier who provided just that in 2003-04 was power forward Carlos Boozer. Boozer's intensity and willingness to "do the dirty work" complemented James well.

"Carlos Boozer is a guy who worships Karl Malone as a player—that lunch box, blue-collar mentality," said Jeff Sack. "Carlos is not a guy who's really looking for the headlines, per se. He knows what his role is."

"Booz, to me," said Austin Carr, "was basically the heart of the team because he did the dirty work, the stick-your-nose-in-there kind of work, night in, night out. He was better than

Carlos Boozer throws down a hard dunk. (AP/WWP)

a dirty work guy, though, because the numbers he produced were all-star numbers."

Many observers felt Boozer was a little on the heavy side while at Duke University. Apparently, Boozer agreed, because he shed 30 pounds before his rookie season of 2002-03.

"He was much more able to be running the floor, getting up and down, going after rebounds two or three times, those kind of things," Carr continued.

However, there were those who thought Boozer was undersized, as well. Paul Silas was among them. He felt Boozer's tenacity and approach to the game more than made up for it.

"He just believes he's good, and he's going to go out and prove it," Silas said. "The defining moment for him was the game in Utah when he scored 32 points and had 20 rebounds and, from then on, he just took off. I had spoken to him prior to that and told him, 'You've got to find a way to be successful; I can't tell you, you find the way,' and I think he found his niche that game, and he was straight ahead from then on."

Unleash the Beast

Boozer may have been an animal on the court—emotional and vocal, too—but in the locker room and off the court, he was a pure gentleman.

"It's like his tattoo says: 'Unleash the beast,'" Tad Carper said. "After a game, you'd ask him about some dunk or rebound, and he'd just look over and say, 'I had to unleash the beast on that one.'"

Overrated?

Not everyone was quite as complimentary. One individual who felt Boozer was a little overrated was Bill Livingston, who believed "Booz" lacked some "oomph" on the defensive end.

"There were lots of times," Livingston said, "where an [opposing player] would break down from the guards and come in, and Z would come over to contest the shot. If the guy missed to the long side, Boozer got the rebound because he seldom rotated over to take cover for Z. [Cavaliers television play-by-play announcer] Michael Reghi would be raving about another double-double for Boozer. I think he's a little undersized to [go up against] the very top power forwards. But they got him at 35 [overall in the 2002 draft], and he's been a tremendous find for that position."

ZYDRUNAS ILGAUSKAS
Surprise, Surprise, Surprise

Another Cavalier who played a vital role in complementing LeBron James in 2003-04 was center Zydrunas Ilgauskas. Ilgauskas enjoyed a rebirth as a defensive force and continued his comeback from numerous foot surgeries, most recently on his left foot in February 2001. He impressed quite a few people with his play, including Bill Livingston.

"Z surprised me a lot," Livingston said. "I'm very happy for him. He's been through a lot. He could've quit. No one would have blamed him if he had retired. It had to be a tremendous ordeal, and I have a lot of respect for him. He is legitimately one of the handful of top centers in the league now—it's a center-barren universe, yes—but there's no denying that he has a game. He's never going to be the player that he was before the foot surgeries, but he's pretty good."

D for Z

Ilgauskas's defensive performance in 2003–04 was tremendous. It very well may have been the best defense Z has ever played. It took a while, though, for early on he was still acclimating himself to Paul Silas's system.

"He wasn't familiar," said Bruce Drennan, "with how many minutes he was going to get. He wasn't used to it, he wasn't comfortable with it, but once he caught on—and he's got a great attitude—that's the most effective he's played. And you could tell his intensity level was higher, too."

"Z was not finishing games in the fourth quarter because he wasn't playing any defense," Bob Karlovec said. "Once he

TURNAROUND

THE 2003-04 CAVALIERS MORE THAN DOUBLED THEIR WIN TOTAL FROM THE SEASON BEFORE (17 TO 35) AND WON MORE GAMES THAN ANY CAVS TEAM IN SIX YEARS. THE CAVALIERS ARE THE ONLY TEAM IN FRANCHISE HISTORY TO MORE THAN DOUBLE THE VICTORY TOTAL FROM THE PREVIOUS SEASON. THE 18-WIN IMPROVEMENT IS SECOND ALL-TIME IN CAVALIERS HISTORY IN BIGGEST SEASON-TO-SEASON TURNAROUND, BEHIND ONLY THE 1991-92 TEAM WHOSE 57 WINS WERE 24 MORE THAN THE SEASON PRIOR. THE 18-GAME IMPROVEMENT ALSO RANKED AS THE THIRD BIGGEST IMPROVEMENT FROM 2002-03 IN THE NBA, BEHIND ONLY DENVER AND MEMPHIS.

started playing defense and giving Silas more of a total package, he was able to be more of a presence offensively and defensively down the stretch."

Z's Renewed Zest

Ilgauskas played with a passion in 2003–04 not seen from him since his first full season with the Cavs, if ever. One reason for the "new and improved" Z was the fact that '03–04 was his second straight season without injury, giving him more self-assurance.

"And I know," said Austin Carr, "because I went through an injury like that. It just boosts your confidence. And you can see him making some moves that he started to make when he was first here before the injuries began. He's starting to reverse pivot, do spin moves, put the ball behind his back, and that's because confidence in that [left] foot was coming back."

Not only was playing minus pain a plus for Z, so was the arrival of point guard Jeff McInnis. Ilgauskas started off a little slow but picked it up when McInnis came aboard.

"The pace of the game was so slow early on," Silas said, "and Z just kind of played into that. Once we got Jeff, the pace really quickened and Z's game really picked up. He became a better rebounder, he became a better offensive player. I had been trying to get him not to play straight up and down, to bend his knees, when he played offensively and defensively. He started doing those things. And a lot was due to the fact that J-Mac would come down, find him, run pick-and-rolls with him, and just take advantage of the wonderful skills that Z has.

"Z is one of the most skilled centers I've ever had. He just has to play with emotion all the time and, of course, when the pace of the game is slow, it's tough for a big man to do that. But he's a guy who works as diligently as anybody on his game. He's a keeper."

Besides the fact that he was healthy and had a true point guard out front, perhaps the most glaring reason for Ilgauskas's improved play was the presence of LeBron James.

"I think LeBron just totally renewed Z's enthusiasm for the game and his willingness to work," said Rick Noland, adding that Silas's stern approach helped too. "Z developed a lot of bad habits during the losing years, but all that changed last year. Silas benched him a few times, got his attention.

"Prior to LeBron and Silas getting there, they couldn't get Ilgauskas to play defense, get a rebound, or pass the ball. If you threw it into him, you pretty much knew he was going to shoot it."

Terry Pluto echoed Noland's sentiments.

"Z used to shoot the ball every time he got it before because he thought nobody would throw it to him," Pluto said. "If he threw it back out, he'd never see it again. He played that way early in the year, and that's when he was sitting down, and suddenly he began to realize, 'No, it's a different team, and they have a different coach.'"

Someone else who noticed the positive change in Ilgauskas was Mark Osowski.

"He is simply a seasoned all-star center with a tremendous work ethic. And that was contagious to the other players," Osowski said. "He really was diligent and dedicated in his workouts, and it showed in practice and in games."

Noland believes the Cavaliers' plan all along was to release Ilgauskas when his contract expires after the 2004–05 season, and use that [salary] cap room to sign someone else. However, Z's play last season may have changed that thinking.

"He meant so much to them," Noland said, "that I think now they're looking at signing him for five or six more years."

Zydrunas Ilgauskas has quite a jump shot. (AP/WWP)

He Can Shoot, Too

Not many centers can sink 20-foot jumpers. Ilgauskas is one who can, making him extremely tough to match up with.

"Z is taller than most of his opponents, so he can shoot over them," said Ira Newble. "And his touch is so soft. I was working out with him during the off season, and I was impressed because he was making more shots than me. He was out there draining his threes! I'm like, 'Man, Z!'"

Concerns

Although Ilgauskas's play improved by leaps and bounds, his track record when it comes to a clean bill of health isn't exactly enviable. With as many surgeries as he has endured and as many games as he has missed, it is difficult to merely file away to memory his injury-marred past.

"His feet will always be an issue with me, and it's always going to hang over his head," Kenny Roda said. "So you have to wonder what will happen after the '04-05 season when his contract is up. He and Gordon Gund have a very strong bond, so I know Gordon wants to keep him. But I don't think he is an absolute, 100-percent necessary piece for this team to win a championship.

"I have my concerns about him defensively as well."

JEFF McINNIS
Sigh of Relief

When point guard Jeff McInnis arrived in late January in a trade with the Portland Trail Blazers, it put a huge smile on the

OPPONENTS ON LEBRON

"LEBRON IS DEFINITELY VERY GIFTED. IT'S HARD TO LIVE UP TO A LOT OF HYPE, BUT I THINK HE'S DONE A PRETTY DECENT JOB. BUT HE'S 19 YEARS OLD, AND HE HAS A LOT OF WORK AHEAD OF HIM. HOPEFULLY, HE'LL CONTINUE TO SURROUND HIMSELF WITH THE RIGHT PEOPLE WHO CAN HELP HIM WITH HIS BASKETBALL SKILLS AND ALSO HIS OFF-THE-COURT KNOWLEDGE. HE'S A REAL QUALITY YOUNG KID, AND HE'S DEFINITELY ONE OF THE GUYS WITH YAO (MING) AND CARMELO (ANTHONY) WHO ARE THE FUTURE OF THE NBA."

—*Steve Francis*, Houston Rockets

face of Paul Silas, for he would no longer have to start LeBron James at point guard.

"Jeff has played the point all his life," Silas said. "That's what he knows, that's what he does, and I think he really flourished at that point. He started to understand the game and how he fit a lot better."

"The Maestro"

Austin Carr called McInnis "The Maestro," the one who conducts the orchestra.

"He does it all," Carr said. "The team responds to his personality that he's a feisty in-your-face kind of guy. He's a bet-

Jeff McInnis takes charge in his first game with Cleveland. (AP/WWP)

ter outside shooter than I thought he was, but he really understands the game. He knows players and knows when to get
them the ball and how to get them the ball. He keeps everybody into the game."

This Is My Chance

McInnis had toiled in relative obscurity with four teams during the preceding seven years. During that period, he also
resorted to playing in Greece and in the Continental
Basketball Association. This was his opportunity to show his
stuff, to prove he had what it takes to succeed in the NBA.

"A guy like Jeff McInnis," Mike Snyder said, "just looked
around and said, 'I'm ready for it, and I'm gonna do it right.'
Silas has brought that out of him. McInnis apparently always
wanted to play for [Sikes], and now he's getting his chance.
He's certainly made a world of difference to this team."

Chapter 5

THE COACH

RESTORING ORDER

Paul Silas brought to the Cavaliers a wealth of experience, including more than seven seasons as a head coach and 16 years as a tough-as-nails front-court player who had a nose for the ball. He was twice an all-star and played on three NBA championship teams.

Silas has a stern approach as a head coach, too. His no-nonsense style impacted in a big way a young team chock-full of players accustomed to a more laid-back climate during the Cavaliers' coaching carousel in recent years. Silas laid down the law from the start by benching notables Carlos Boozer, Zydrunas Ilgauskas and, yes, even LeBron James at times.

"I have tremendous respect for Paul Silas," Terry Pluto said. "There are only about 12 coaches who NBA players respect, and he's one of them. He's been around and, even if you disagree with him tactically, I don't think anybody ever thought there was a point where the team was out of control or that he didn't have a handle on what was going on. And if you've

Paul Silas. (Mark Goldman/Icon SMI)

watched what has been happening here for the previous years, that was not the case."

The players responded well and, after a trade that sent "me-first" Ricky Davis to the Celtics, Silas molded the team into a competitive unit. Then, after a deal that brought a sorely needed point guard in Jeff McInnis to town, the Cavs played themselves into a position in which a playoff berth was a distinct possibility. They fell just short in the end, but Silas's presence has undoubtedly restored order in Cavalier Land.

TESTING, TESTING

Typically, there are a handful of games per season in which players take the night off, fail to show up, according to Terry Pluto, no matter the team. How many games that amounts to depends upon the impact of the coach. And Paul Silas's presence clearly impressed upon his players that an attitude of that nature would not be tolerated.

"They didn't have 18-20 games like that as in the past," Pluto said. "The defense, to me, kind of went downhill at the end of the year, but that was a big improvement. Offensively, in general, you always had people shooting at the right basket and generally taking, for the most part, pretty good shots. And I don't mean just Ricky Davis. There were a lot of guys taking bad shots [in previous years]. But the players have to trust the coach to have enough guts to insist that there's order. I think they were testing Paul just to say, 'Is he going to put any teeth into his orders?'"

MY WAY OR THE PINE-WAY

When Paul Silas was hired as Cavaliers head coach, he inherited a situation not unlike a teacher taking over a classroom where there had been nothing but substitutes for three years.

"[The players] didn't know how to react to a guy who was going to not only act like he's in charge," Terry Pluto said, "but be in charge, and have a four-year contract for $18 million to prove it. That's why, early in the year, he was making moves where he was benching people and suspending people and, frankly, not so much coaching to win games but to establish order.

A lot of fans didn't get it, failed to comprehend the new coach's blueprint for success. But there were some who got it.

"I knew exactly what he was doing," said Pluto. "It was right. It was a mess. It was a bigger mess than people know because there had been no discipline. And the only thing NBA players react to is not playing. I mean, you can't fine them, where it means anything. You write 'fine,' they take it off their taxes."

"He does it to get you to understand what he's looking for," expanded Austin Carr, who believes Silas is the perfect coach for this team because of his "old school" ways. "He lets you know that he's got control of the minutes. You get playing time on your merits."

Silas commanded respect from his players, and got it.

"His teams were prepared, and they, by and large, played hard," Bill Livingston said. "The team showed more inner toughness than they had shown in years. I think they were barely coached the two or three years prior to last season. John Lucas just wasn't the coach for a young team, Keith Smart was a puppet of [Jim] Paxson's, and Randy Wittman had pretty much lost the team by his last year."

MUST-WIN SITUATION

Even with the early struggles, Jim Paxson noticed a subtle change in the atmosphere. He attributed it to Paul Silas.

"Even though we were losing," Paxson said, "he wasn't accepting it, and wouldn't let the players accept it. And that was really key because, when you come off a 17-win season, LeBron or no LeBron, you don't want that to be an environment that lingers. But I think Paul kind of set the standard, and we made a couple of trades that helped us through that."

AIRWAVES TO THE LeBRONTH DEGREE

THE CAVALIERS' BROADCASTING DEPARTMENT EXPERIENCED SEVERAL INCREASES IN 2003-04:

- LOCAL TELEVISION RATINGS WERE UP MORE THAN 300 PERCENT FROM 2002-03.
- EIGHTY GAMES, THE MOST IN FRANCHISE HISTORY, WERE TELEVISED.
- SIXTEEN GAMES WERE NATIONALLY TELEVISED, MORE THAN THE PRIOR 10 SEASONS COMBINED.
- THE CAVALIERS TELEVISION NETWORK EXPANDED FROM THREE TO EIGHT STATIONS.
- THE CAVALIERS RADIO NETWORK DOUBLED FROM EIGHT TO 16 STATIONS.

"THREE" TEAMS

The 2003–04 Cavaliers started out very young and then gained some experience with two significant trades as the season progressed. Paul Silas, in effect, coached three different teams, two of them without benefit of a training camp.

"The one he coached with a training camp was the first one," said Bob Karlovec. "That's the one that got off to the very poor start because he had to have LeBron basically playing the point. That's when he realized that is not the best place for him. So they made the first trade to get some more veteran players in there, and they played better, they played closer to .500. Then, of course, they made the last deal, moving [Darius] Miles to Portland to get Jeff McInnis, and that was the

OPPONENTS ON LEBRON

"WHEN YOU LOOK AT THE ALL-AROUND PLAYER, AND DON'T JUST LOOK AT THE HYPE, BUT LOOK AT SUBSTANCE AND WHAT HE DOES, HE CAN DRIBBLE, PASS AND SHOOT. THOSE ARE THE THREE THINGS THAT MAKE A GREAT PLAYER AT ANY LEVEL. DOUBLE THAT WITH HIS ATHLETIC EXPLOSIVENESS AND ALL THE OTHER THINGS. IF YOU KNOCK IT ALL BACK TO THE BASICS OF THE GAME, YOU WOULD BE HARD-PRESSED TO FIND TOO MANY GUYS RIGHT NOW IN THE LEAGUE WHO CAN DO THOSE SKILLS."

—*Scott Skiles,* Chicago Bulls head coach

last piece of the puzzle, at least for last season, to put them on a winning track."

DOUBTS

Not everyone saw Silas as the Cavs' savior. Hal Lebovitz is one media member who has his reservations about the Cavaliers' head coach.

"Whether Paul Silas is the right coach to lead this team to a championship is still up for debate. He didn't come close to proving that in his previous coaching jobs," said Lebovitz, who writes sports for *The News-Herald* in Lake County, Ohio, and is a former long time sports editor of *The Plain Dealer* in Cleveland.

Chapter 6

THE SEASON

B.L. (BEFORE LEBRON)

T he Cavaliers had gone through some very tough times in the five years leading up to the 2003-04 season, especially the season before when they won just 15 games. Gordon Gund shed some light on reasons why the team was so unsuccessful. Besides the fact that the Cavaliers had difficulty in settling in on the right head coach, Gund pointed to a pair of big men whose problems affected the team in big ways but were worlds apart in nature.

"We had a player who we thought would really add a great deal, that being Shawn Kemp," he said. "Shawn went in a different direction. We also had a center [Zydrunas Ilgauskas] who we still happen to think very highly of but who had foot problems during that period of time. Just as we'd get started off to a good run, he would have another problem, and that set us way back, so we had difficulties there.

Gund then brought up a third big man and spoke of his saga.

"Brad Daugherty had to cut his career very short just before that five-year period," Gund added. "Otherwise, since he was only 28 when his injury happened, we would've had him for a lot of that. He was already a five-time all-star. I think he could've been a Hall of Fame player had he continued."

THE PREMIERE
Springtime in October

The 2003-04 season began with a bang as the Cavaliers gave the star-studded Sacramento Kings all they could handle before falling, 106-92, in sold-out ARCO Arena before a national television audience. The atmosphere that night instilled feelings in Mark Osowski that are usually reserved for April, May, and June. The excitement level was that high.

"With all eyes watching our team," Osowski said, "there was just a feeling of electricity in the building. It felt like when you come out for the playoffs and come out of the locker room."

Simply Dazzling

There were many who believed LeBron James would never be able to live up to the incredible hype. There were those who took it a step further; they felt James would fail miserably in the opener against the Kings.

Not only did LeBron not fail, he was spectacular. The rookie dazzled the doubters by scoring 25 points, dishing out nine assists, and grabbing six rebounds.

"LeBron played under some very adverse circumstances out in Sacramento," said Joe Tait. "That crowd is one of the toughest in the league, and the Kings are also one of the better teams in the league. He stepped right up and did his thing. So it was apparent right off the top of the page that he was going to be something special."

Paul Silas thought James would struggle somewhat. He certainly did not expect him to shoot like he did.

"He just mesmerized everybody," Silas said. "He shot it well, he assisted and, at that time, I had the ball in his hands [as point guard]. He handled everything so well. We got off to a slow start, and then we got back in the game and actually lost it coming down the stretch. I just said, 'Wow, if this is the way this is going to be, this kid is just going to set the world on fire.' I had never expected, or really seen, anything like that."

The telephone rang in the Mike Snyder household after the game, which did not end until well after midnight.

"It was [WTAM-AM 1100 talk-show host] Mike Trivisonno," Snyder recalled. "He was going, 'Can you believe this guy's ours?'"

Bill Livingston remembered not hitting the sack until the wee hours of the morning. He couldn't tear himself away from his P.C.

"I remember watching that game on TV and staying up until two in the morning e-mailing with other basketball-nut friends of mine," he said. "I couldn't believe [LeBron] had been that good, and I couldn't believe he was going to be playing here for the foreseeable future."

PD Reader?

Livingston recalled a certain play by LeBron in the opener that made for quite the coincidence. It was a left-hand finger roll he made, which Livingston had never seen.

"In fact," Livingston said, "I had written a column urging him to learn to become a bank shooter and to develop his left hand. It was the only time I saw him shoot with his left hand.

I wondered where in the hell that came from. It was almost Gervin-esque."

Over-hyped?

It is easy to build up something to the point where it is impossible for the end result to equal expectations. The opener in Sacramento was hyped big time. And although most people felt the game did match expectations, there were those who were not as impassioned.

"[The opener] was a big event," Terry Pluto said, "but it's not like somebody thought this was the second coming of FDR or whoever your favorite politician was. I think this was just a very interesting player to go watch. It was like when Julius Erving came to town many years ago after the ABA went to pasture, or maybe the first visit of Jordan."

"I think winning the lottery was bigger than opening night," added Greg Brinda. "It was almost anticlimactic."

PLANET CLEVELAND

The Cavaliers lost their first five games, including the home opener against the Carmelo Anthony-led Nuggets that caused the biggest stir over a Denver team playing in Cleveland since John Elway led the Broncos over the Browns 17 years earlier in the AFC Championship game. The atmosphere was electrifying.

"We had this horde of people camping out the night before to be first in line," Len Komoroski recalled. "Those tickets were gold in the marketplace, with Carmelo Anthony coming in. It had a Hollywood type of feel—almost surreal—because of the amount of star power that was there. You had Phil

Knight sitting courtside, and different movie stars who were in the house."

Even ESPN was there, broadcasting the game nationally.

"You couldn't go out the exit we normally do," said Bill Livingston. "You had to go all the way across the end of the court because 'Stuie' [ESPN personality Stuart Scott] was back there yelling, 'Boo-yah!' on camera. And unfortunately, today, with all that they've done to create hype and stuff, ESPN is kind of one of the validators that this is a big-time event. It had kind of the feel of a heavyweight title fight, although it turned out to be one of the bad heavyweight title fights, a heavyweight title fight of today's fighters."

Added Terry Pluto, "They hadn't had a big basketball game at Gund Arena, I would argue, ever, since the move [from the Coliseum in Richfield almost a decade earlier]. So that was a big deal."

"Just arriving at the arena and seeing the excitement, you could definitely sense there was a different type of buzz in the air that night," David Kelly said. "I mean, Ken Griffey Jr., was there. I think Jay-Z was there. They were sitting right there courtside. You could tell it was definitely different than any other home opener I had experienced here in Cleveland."

Opening night was more about people wanting to see LeBron James than a basketball game. It was not a traditional basketball atmosphere.

"Everybody was just taking pictures of him and staring at him," Chad Estis said. "During introductions, the whole crowd was on its feet."

SLOW START

It took six games for the Cavaliers to notch their first victory of 2003-04, a 111-98 triumph over Washington on November

8 at Gund Arena. They improved to 4-7 but then dropped eight straight games, eventually falling to 6-19. Paul Silas was perplexed by his inability to stop the bleeding.

"I wondered about our slow start," he said, "because things didn't jell like I thought they would. I had Darius [Miles], Ricky [Davis], and LeBron starting with Z and Booz, and I thought we were going to be very athletic, teams were going to have a tough time matching up with us, and it just didn't click. I wondered whether or not we were going to be able to sustain anything or not. We got off to the horrible start on the road, and I kind of wondered, 'Hey, are we ever going to win a game?' I knew we were going to win one eventually, but when?"

THE IRA INCIDENT

The Cavaliers had just lost to the Atlanta Hawks on a late-November Saturday evening in Georgia. Ira Newble, who had played for the Hawks the two previous seasons, was geared up to play well not only against his former team, but in front of several friends and family members in attendance. Unfortunately for Newble, he received little playing time and was not pleased about it.

"Looking back," Paul Silas said, "it was just a miscalculation on my part. But after the game I mentioned something to him, and he walked in the locker room and just kind of ignored me. A shouting match ensued.

"I tell the guys all the time that it's never going to be a bed of roses between me and them, we're going to have our moments. And that certainly was one where Ira and I went at it—and I went at it with a lot of the guys throughout the year—but the one thing I don't do is hold grudges. After it's over, it's over. The next day, Ira apologized, and apologized to the team, and today he's one of my favorite players. He, probably more than anyone, wants to win. He'll do anything it takes to win, and I just love him for that."

Newble said it was a simple matter of miscommunication between coach and player. The two were not in tune with one another.

"Basically, we were trying to learn each other's styles," he said. "I was new to him, he was new to me. We were both competitive, and we didn't really see eye to eye at first on what each other was doing. So all that kind of came to a head in Atlanta. Everybody was frustrated because we were on a losing streak and also we lost to one of the worst teams in the league."

IT'S BEEN REAL, RICK
Addition by Subtraction

A December trade with the team struggling significantly changed the course of the season. The Cavaliers shipped pouting Ricky Davis, along with Chris Mihm, Michael Stewart, and a future second-round draft pick to the Celtics for Eric Williams, Tony Battie, and Kedrick Brown.

The move allowed James to take charge and become "The Man," the very reason the Cavs drafted him. Davis was the Cavs' leading scorer the year before and was accustomed to being the "go-to guy." He was unwilling to play second fiddle to James, which hindered the chemistry of the team. That was the catalyst for the trade. The Cavaliers won eight of their next 18.

"There are different types of jealousy," Jim Paxson said. "With Ricky Davis, I think he realized LeBron was going to be a great player and everything else. And I think he was okay with all the attention LeBron got in certain ways. It's just, on the floor, Ricky's the type of player who wants the ball, and one of LeBron's strengths is having the ball and making other players better. So I think that was hard for Ricky to deal with. I think it was just Ricky kind of feeling like he could do it all and didn't know how to balance that."

Before the season even started, Bill Livingston was convinced that Davis had to go. He felt Ricky was that much of a hindrance.

"I thought [Ricky] was the dumbest good player I'd ever seen," Livingston said. "I just think he would not have accepted being a secondary player, and he just did stupid things down the crunch of games. It was very difficult to win with Ricky Davis. It doesn't mean he's a bad guy or anything like that, I just think he's a loser."

Ira Newble added his two cents' worth. He felt Davis's youth played a role in his reluctance to give way to LeBron as the team's main man.

"Ricky's a young player, and it was hard for him. He hadn't really been put in that type of position before," said Newble, who added that the deal likely helped both the Cavs and Davis himself. "We got more defensive-minded guys and Ricky, who was frustrated, got to go to a different situation because he's used to having the ball a lot."

Paul Silas felt the trade helped the Cavaliers because they got players who were more in tune with what the team needed.

"We got some guys in who had been there before," Silas said, "who understood, were winners, and we began to turn things around. I think that was kind of a defining moment for our ball club also."

It Could Have Worked

Whereas most observers thought the trade was beneficial to the Cavaliers, not everyone felt that way. Rick Noland was one of the very few.

"I still think Ricky Davis was worth keeping," he said, "and I'm in a small, small, small minority on that one."

IT'S A START

The Cavaliers defeated the Philadelphia 76ers, 88-81, on December 19, 2003, in Philadelphia. The victory halted a 34–game road losing streak by the Cavs. The streak, which dated back to January 13 of that year, was tied for the second longest in NBA history.

It was a huge win, one that set the tone for the remainder of the season, as the Cavaliers won 12 of their last 28 road games and were even within sniffing distance of the playoffs until the last week of the season.

"It was a nice win," said Austin Carr, "because they had that road albatross around their neck."

It was also vital to the future of the team.

"If you're going to win a championship some day," Carr added, "you first have to learn how to win at home and, second, you have to learn how win on the road because, in the playoffs, all your games are not at home.

CHRISTMAS "MAGIC"

The Cavaliers played their first Christmas Day game in 14 years when they opposed Orlando in the TD Waterhouse Centre. The Cavs lost, 113-101, in overtime. This matchup was scheduled, not because of the teams, but due to the first ever meeting between LeBron James and Tracy McGrady. The duel was highly anticipated and didn't disappoint. James was spectacular, scoring 34 points and dishing out six assists. McGrady was even better, amassing 41 points, eight rebounds, and 11 assists.

"LeBron and Tracy McGrady had a shootout," Austin Carr said. "It was fabulous. That was a great game."

"I'll never forget LeBron's shot over McGrady from the deep corner," said Bill Livingston, "that went about 20 feet in the air."

JUST WHAT THE DOCTOR ORDERED

Notable deal number two occurred in late January when the Cavaliers shipped Darius Miles to Portland for guard Jeff McInnis and throw-in Ruben Boumtje Boumtje. The season took off from there. The Cavs went 21-19 the rest of the way.

McInnis was a true point guard and possessed the ability to make things happen. He became the third piece of the puzzle, helping LeBron James pave the way to a competitive season for the Cavs.

"When they first got McInnis," said Bruce Drennan, "you could see the difference in the chemistry immediately, the distributor and penetrator that he is, especially after he learned the strategy and philosophies of [Paul] Silas. He's a pro's pro, and adapted to it very quickly."

Added Ira Newble, "It was a different look for us and a look we needed. Jeff's a talented point guard, very good at getting everybody involved. It worked for us because they moved LeBron to the two [guard] and made him more of just a scorer. He could get out on the break more and let Jeff create and get everybody else involved. Not to mention Jeff can score, and that really helped too."

Newble believes, had McInnis not been injured down the stretch, the Cavs would have been in the playoffs.

"The season was already special from how we turned it around and fought so hard," he said, "but that would have put an exclamation point on it."

THE INDIANA GAME
We Belong

The game against the Indiana Pacers on March 14 was one of two home games that stood out as most memorable of the season. The Cavaliers were on a five-game winning streak and positioning themselves for a playoff run. The Pacers had won seven straight and boasted the best record in the NBA. The Cavs played perhaps their finest game of the season. They won, 107-104, in a thriller of monumental proportions that allowed them to hang onto the sixth playoff position in the Eastern Conference—but barely. Their record stood at 30-36.

"Indiana jumped out ahead. They were getting lay ups early," Jim Paxson recalled. "But we played as good a game as we could play the last three and a half quarters and ended up winning by three. That game in itself, for me, was the highlight of the season."

"It was probably one of the more exciting games that I was at last year," said David Kelly. "It was against, obviously, a team that was considered to be the dominant team then. The Cavs were on a roll at the time but were down late in the fourth. The way they just pulled together and pulled that game out and beat Indiana was very impressive."

It is not as if the Pacers were not up to par. They played a fine game. They shot well over 50 percent from the field. The Cavs, though, matched them point for point.

"The Cavaliers stepped up," said Bob Karlovec. "They just flat out beat Indiana that day, and LeBron was almost unstop-

LeBron James was an unstoppable force against the Pacers in the Cavs' 107-104 victory. Here he drives around forward Jermaine O'Neal. (AP/WWP)

LeBron's Career Night

L eBron James had his finest game as a professional on March 27, 2004, at home against New Jersey. James scored a career-high 41 points, dished out a career-best 13 assists, and grabbed six rebounds in the Cavaliers' 107-104 win.

pable at times. I think it was the best game the Cavaliers played all season. It was an outstanding basketball game."

Some Kind of Wonderful

The atmosphere was electric inside Gund Arena. It may have been the most glorious game in terms of atmosphere since the Cavaliers moved there in 1994. To Mike Snyder, it was even akin to some of the good ol' days at the Coliseum in Richfield.

"It was certainly comparable to past playoff experiences," Snyder said, "whether it was the Price-Daugherty years or the Miracle year."

Passing the Ar-Test

Pacers forward Ron Artest was in LeBron James's face all day, bumping him, hoping he'd lose his cool. LeBron would not buckle.

"LeBron just kept coming back harder and harder, and kept going to the basket and going to the basket, no matter how many times he was knocked down," said Rick Noland. "He'd just get back up, make the free throws, and go back again. That was one of the knocks on LeBron at times, that he didn't go to the hole enough. That night, he just did it over and over and over."

Foretelling the Future?

There were a handful of times when the Cavaliers provided fans with gems—games in which they could not have looked better. The Pacers game may have topped the charts.

"I think, from a standpoint of what this team thinks it might be able to do," said Karlovec, "that was the game that gave everyone a taste. That was the game that was kind of a look into the future, so to speak, as to what this team might be able to accomplish down the road."

Sunday Memories

The Pacers game was one of four Sunday afternoon games the Cavaliers played in 2003-04. It put Kelly in the mood for reminiscing.

"It brought back memories from the late '80s and early '90s," he reflected, "when all those Sunday afternoon games they used to have down at Richfield during the playoff runs were on."

Radio Days Return

Unfortunately, for anyone who was not inside Gund Arena that memorable afternoon, the game was one of just two on the schedule that was not televised.

"It was the best game of the season," recalled Karlovec, "and it's kind of ironic that the best game of the year was one that the only people who actually saw it were the 20-some thousand who were in Gund Arena that day."

"It was foolishly not included on the ABC-TV menu," Livingston added, "and began at some oddball hour (3 p.m.). It was probably LeBron's best game, the game that nobody saw."

"It made owning a ticket really pretty special," Kelly said.

THE NEW JERSEY GAME
LeBron Takes Charge

Some two weeks after the Cavaliers' exhilarating victory over the Indiana Pacers came the second installment of "Memorable Cavs Victories by 107-104 Scores." On March 27, the Cavaliers, minus an injured Jeff McInnis, limped into a game against the formidable New Jersey Nets. And just as two weeks before against the Pacers, the Cavs, led by LeBron James's 41 points and 13 assists, pulled the upset. They did so by, remarkably, the exact same score. This game was the Cavs' one and only victory in a 12-game stretch.

"The Nets game was just absolutely unbelievable," said Mike Snyder. "LeBron single-handedly won it. He just took the game over and wouldn't be denied. It was just an incredible performance on both ends of the floor."

"At one point," added Rick Noland, "LeBron had about three or four straight dunks in a span of a minute and a half, one where he took the ball behind his back and split two defenders and then just went up and slammed it. He had a couple lob dunks, too. In fact, the best dunk might have been one he missed when somebody threw the ball about four feet behind the backboard, and he tried to windmill it home. It slammed off the side of the rim. The crowd went just as nuts on that one as on the one he made. For him to even get close to it, it took a superhuman effort."

Proud to Be a Cavs Fan

When Snyder conducted his on-court postgame interview with James, the crowd could hear for itself the young star's poise, and ease, with the media.

"LeBron just understands the situation," Snyder said. "He knows, in that interview, he's talking to the fans who are in the building, and he always seems to say the right thing when he's there, and make the people feel good. He addresses them and thanks them and so forth. That night gave me goose bumps, to see a guy wearing a Cavaliers jersey be able to go out and do that. It was just incredible."

PLAYOFF PUSH
"March"-ing to the Postseason?

The Cavaliers had dug themselves into an 0-5 hole to begin the season. By a week before Christmas, they were 6-19. But with LeBron James leading the way, and with the help of two significant trades, they found themselves with a record of 24-36 and on the cusp of playoff contention heading into a home game against the Atlanta Hawks on March 3. Some two weeks and a seven-game winning streak later, the Cavs were caught up in a torrid chase for the final three playoff spots in the Eastern Conference.

"There was a sizzle to the team during the streak," said Mike Snyder. "You could just feel it building there. Things really came alive."

"That was pretty awesome," Paul Silas said, "when we got on that seven-game winning streak and played some really, really good basketball. It just shows me that we're capable. Looking at the team as a whole, you really begin to appreciate what they did, what they had to come through, and still had a chance at the end. It showed me a lot of character that these guys were able to do that."

Bad "Break"

An injury to point guard Jeff McInnis in a blowout of the Chicago Bulls on March 16 headed the Cavs on a downhill slide. They lost 11 of their next 12 games and dropped out of playoff contention. In the end, the team wound up 35-47, barely missing the postseason and finishing one game (two with the tiebreaker) behind the Boston Celtics for the eighth and final playoff berth.

"The Celtics did come on when they needed to at the end," said Bob Karlovec, "and played just well enough to be able to hold off the Cavaliers. And the Cavaliers played just badly enough that, even when they went on that teeny little run at the end [when they won three straight to end the season], it wasn't quite enough."

Jim Paxson was astonished at how quickly things changed after McInnis's injury.

"LeBron got a viral infection over the next three games," he said. "He wasn't 100 percent, but he played through it. So you lose to Utah, Detroit kicks our butt, and then Phoenix beats us [all at home]. We were really flat that [Suns] game.

"So, from the elation from one week, nine days later it was ... it hurt that McInnis was out and not 100 percent, but my feeling was that if we would've beaten Phoenix, Toronto, and Golden State, all games we lost at home late in the year, we would've been in the playoffs."

Learning to Crawl

More than half of all NBA teams qualify for the postseason, resulting in widespread yawning from fans in many cities. Not so with Cleveland and the Cavaliers, according to Austin Carr.

"The playoffs aren't the easiest thing to make when you come from where we came from," said Carr. "We came from the dregs of the league to being one of the most feared teams that didn't make the playoffs. Nobody wanted to play us in the playoffs because they knew we had the size. We didn't have the experience, but we had the size, and anything can happen."

No Excuses Allowed

"Not making the playoffs," said Terry Pluto, "showed some weaknesses on the team and showed that, when it came right down to having to win some games, they couldn't do it. I think McInnis was probably 70 percent of it, but you have to figure out how to win some games without him. I'm still kind of dumbfounded at exactly what the reason was [for not advancing to the postseason]. But it wasn't just the injury. Jeff McInnis is very good, but he's not Oscar Robertson, so let's put that in context."

"The unfortunate thing," Bill Livingston said, "was when it was there to be taken, it didn't happen, and [the Cavs] blamed it all on the injury to McInnis, but LeBron can play the point, too. My feeling is that they were kind of worn down. They had a lot of close games, and that takes a lot out of you, and they won more than their share."

GROUND RULE DOUBLE

When an NBA team—or any team, for that matter—doubles its win total from the previous season, it is usually cause for celebration. When the 2003-04 Cavaliers achieved the feat (and one game more), many people did rejoice. On the other hand, there were those who didn't. Bill Livingston was one.

"I wasn't all that impressed the Cavs doubled their wins," Livingston said, "because they only won 17 the year before. But it's still more than I thought they would do."

BULL'S-EYE ON OUR BACK

Most NBA teams that opposing clubs shoot for have won a championship, or close to it. Even with their improved play, the 2003-04 Cavaliers were nowhere near being an elite team. Why, they didn't even win half their games! In spite of their record, though, the Cavs were directly on other teams' radars.

"Because of all the hype," said Jim Paxson, "and teams not wanting to be the poster child of a dunk of LeBron's on SportsCenter, we had teams come at us every night. Just because of LeBron, everybody was up to play the Cavaliers despite our record. So you maybe didn't get those three or four extra wins per year on nights where some teams maybe don't show up because they underestimate opponents. I think that will help the growth of our team."

BENCH-PRESSED

LeBron James is a great player with unlimited potential. But he is not a magician. He cannot just say, "Voila!" and conjure up a championship. Just like other greats such as Michael Jordan, Magic Johnson and Larry Bird, James will need teammates to step up if the Cavaliers hope to attain championship status.

"You just have one guy and four journeymen," Joe Tait said, "you're not going to win the title. I think we have the foundation for a very good basketball team. I think the most important thing is to bolster the bench. You have to have better production on a night-in, night-out basis off your bench than we had last year. That, in the long run, was the Achilles' heel of the Cavaliers last season."

Bill Livingston took it a step further.

"I thought the whole season was basically about LeBron," he said, "and the improvement of the team was just a nice subplot to that. Once you got past LeBron, McInnis, Boozer, and Z, it was just an amorphous bunch of okay to sub-okay players."

OPPONENTS ON LEBRON

"He's from Ohio—what did you expect? The thing about him that you have to love is his maturity. He doesn't force things. A rookie in his position with all the attention and all the fame could come in and be big-headed, but he's not. If you see how he plays, he really wants to get his teammates involved, and that's the mark of a great player."

—*Jim Jackson*, Houston Rockets

LONG WAY TO GO

Had the Cavaliers managed to qualify for the postseason, it would have made for a nice story, but the fact would have remained that they were still a losing team with a bright future—with the emphasis on "future."

"Let's face it," Greg Brinda said, "they didn't really have a good team. Bottom line, when you're 10–12 games under .500, you're not a good basketball team, you really don't deserve to be in the playoffs. When you're under .500, you're not even mediocre."

TO: SENEGAL

DeSegana Diop didn't contribute much in 2003–04 but was still featured on game program covers and in promotional giveaways. The seven-foot, 280-pound backup center was thrilled to say the least, and wanted his family thousands of miles away to share in his joy.

"We were always packaging 30–40 programs or posters or whatever else," Tad Carper recalled, "to send back to Senegal to his family."

LEBRON MOMENTS (ON COURT)
Eyes in the Back of His Head

There were times when it appeared that James was from another planet in terms of his court awareness. He was a step ahead and left opponents for dead. Paul Silas recalled one particular pass he made in a game against the Chicago Bulls.

"LeBron was on a fast break," Silas said, "and J-Mac got the ball and throws an outlet pass to LeBron. LeBron was going in, there was a man in front of him, and he did this no-look over his head and, BOOM, to Booz, who was running in for the jam. It's the kind of play you just can't fully appreciate until you see it on film. At the time, it's just part of basketball, but when you see it on film, you just go, 'Wow!' And there are just so many little passes and things like that that he made."

Anyone Happen to Have a Video Camera Rolling?

Perhaps LeBron's most remarkable play of the year occurred during a practice session. It was a jaw-dropper of a move that turned everyone's head.

"Somebody threw an [alley]-oop almost half court to LeBron," Ira Newble said.

"Kevin Ollie was back on defense," added Mark Osowski, "and tried to get a deflection on the pass, but it was like LeBron had afterburners. He jumped, he just kept going up, caught the ball, and finished it with two hands.

"Kevin was up there, and then both of them came down in a heap, just tumbling down. Everyone kind of looked at each other and, at that point, you held your breath for a second. LeBron jumped right up and headed back downcourt ready to play defense. Kevin got up, too. It was great. The amazing part was how high LeBron jumped, able to not just catch the ball and control it, but finish on the break with the defender right there."

"It was unbelievable," Newble said, "almost at the top of the backboard. That was one of the most memorable dunks I've ever seen. We all had to stop and think, 'Man, I wish that was during a game so somebody else could see it!'"

He's Our Meal Ticket

During a March 8 game in Atlanta, Cavaliers players showed a semblance of unity not seen from the team in a long time. It stemmed from an incident in which the Hawks' Stephen Jackson pushed LeBron James to the ground.

"He basically hit LeBron," recalled Jeff Sack. "It was kind of a dirty-foul type of thing, and I remember the rest of the [Cavaliers] rushing to his aid and basically saying to Jackson that that was not going to be tolerated. And I was saying to myself, 'Boy, this is a new facet of this Cavaliers team!' that the players would rush to the aid of one of their teammates. No one was worried that he was hurt or anything, just the fact that, 'How dare you attack our player!'"

LeBron Moments (Off Court)
It's a Business

When the Cavaliers traded Darius Miles to the Portland Trail Blazers on January 21, they traded LeBron's best friend on the team. Right after the deal was made, James was asked by Jeff Sack what the move meant to him.

"You could definitely see the sadness in his face," Sack recalled. "But he knew, I think, deep down, it was the best thing for the team. Of course, it certainly did turn out that way."

No Slipping Out the Back Door

Kenny Roda took his son, Cameron, to a late-season Cavaliers game and had VIP passes to boot. This allowed the duo to enjoy food, beverages, and rub shoulders with the high rollers before, during, and after the game in an area near the locker rooms called the VIP Club. The players must pass by to leave the building.

"LeBron signed every autograph for every kid who was there. My son got LeBron's autograph," said Roda. "I think [the Cavs] lost that game too, and that was toward the end of the season. It had been a long year and everything, and LeBron could've escaped somewhere but didn't."

Fan Appreciation

LeBron has that special "something," a combination of charisma and charm that makes people smile. He knows how to work a crowd, and that includes those at Gund Arena.

"I remember the first game he came back after [an ankle injury he suffered]," Bill Livingston recalled, "he didn't play all that well. It was a gutty effort, I mean he certainly wasn't a liability, but it wasn't what he had been before the injury. And it was one of the rare times he was on the postgame interview [with Mike Snyder on WTAM-AM 1100], with the fans at courtside. [LeBron] said, 'Yeah, the injury was bothering me, but these fans, the way they treat me, it just made it really great.'"

Give Me June Jubilation Any Day

As James was doing his best to keep the Cavaliers from falling out of the Eastern Conference playoff race, March Madness was in full bloom in the world of college basketball. It was a world LeBron could have been a part of had he traveled a different road. He was asked if he regretted missing out on "The Big Dance."

"Without hesitation," Kenny Roda recalled, "he said, 'No, this is where I've always wanted to be. I have no regrets whatsoever.'"

My Fault, Coach

LeBron was benched during the first half of the season finale against the Knicks in New York. Silas did it because James was not hustling to get back on defense.

"LeBron came over and was looking at him," Roda recalled. "And Silas said, 'You've got to get back on defense!' And he said LeBron looked at him like, 'What?' And Silas just said, 'Am I wrong?' And LeBron just looked at him and said, 'No,' and understood everything, and then came out and scored the majority of his points in the second half, and they won the game."

Friendly Fire

At the NBA Rookie of the Year award press conference in Cleveland honoring LeBron, player and coach were laughing, ribbing one another. They were just having a good ol' time.

"You could tell it wasn't phony, it wasn't fake, it was true," Kenny Roda said. "LeBron joked, 'Now you see what I had to deal with all year in practice?' because Silas would needle him. And he talked about how Silas said that during his playing days, 'If I would've come down the lane like you did a couple of times this year, I would've knocked you down.' So you can see the relationship is a natural and a friendly one, and a true one."

LeBron James and Coach Silas share a laugh during the 2004 NBA Rookie of the Year press conference at Gund Arena. (AP/WWP)

Thanks, LeBron

In 1970, when Gordon Gund was 30 years old, he was stricken with a progressive degenerative disease of the retina called retinitis pigmentosa that took what remained of his vision. Gund, however, did not let that interfere with his quest for success. A year later, he and his wife became founding members of The Foundation Fighting Blindness, a world-renowned organization based in Baltimore. Gund has gone on to live a richer, fuller life than most people even dream of.

LeBron was asked to do a public service announcement for the foundation, a 30-second spot that ran through the 2003–04 playoffs. He was more than willing.

"[LeBron] urges people," Gund said, "who are affected with retinal degenerative diseases, or who want to help people who are losing their site to these diseases, to contact the foundation. That meant a great deal to me."

THE FUTURE

For the first time in more than a decade, the Cavaliers seem to be headed in the right direction. But the team must also realize that if it does, indeed, fulfill its potential with even greater success, higher expectations will come right along with it.

"We got a bye last year because of where we started from," said Carr. "But I would imagine that the fan base is going to expect higher things, and I know the coaching staff is going to expect higher things because they worked so hard to get to where they are now that they want to take the next step."

According to Larry Pantages, LeBron's third year will be the tell-all season. That will be the year when fans find out if serious success—meaning games in May and June—is on the horizon.

"I'm fond of saying you've got to give an up-and-coming player three years to really get his legs," Pantages said. "And I base that on seeing [ex-Cavalier] Roy Hinson, for example. When the Cavs drafted Roy, he was this skinny kid with long arms, and they put him in at center, and boy, the third year, there were blocked shots, dunks…that was awesome. [Danny] Ferry maybe needed more than three years, Mark Price three years.

"So I'm looking at year two in the LeBron era as just another building block. A great goal would be to make the playoffs, get into the first round. Anything can happen even if you're the eighth seed. But I'm looking at the third year as, 'Now, can we get to 50 wins?' And you get the home court advantage, and then things can happen for you. But you want continuity with the system, you want Silas to really learn the ins and outs. So I think in the third year with Silas and his system, that's when you can say, 'Are we ready now? Do we have some pieces? Do we have the rebounder off the bench? Do we have the enforcer? Do we have the guy who's instant offense?'"

Chapter 7

WHAT A DIFFERENCE
A YEAR MAKES

DULL DAYS, LOSING WAYS

Empty seats. Apathy. Not a pulse. Crowds at Gund Arena were so miniscule during the 2002-03 season, they nearly rivaled those of the Ted Stepien era. The atmosphere surrounding the Cavaliers at Gund Arena was comparable to the mood in a dentist's waiting room.

"The Gund was a funeral parlor for two or three years," said Rick Noland. "They were announcing crowds that were 10, 11, 12,000, and they were lucky if there were 6,000 people in there. They were giving away the tickets and discounting them unbelievably low just to get those people in there. The loudest crowds I heard at Gund Arena before last year were the two or three times I went up there when LeBron was playing with St.V. That place was electric then."

"It is no joke," Bob Karlovec said, "that I used to tell people there were only two times all season in the years leading up to LeBron when I would see excitement at Gund Arena. One was when the Mid-American Conference played their basketball tournament there in March, the other was Cleveland Rockers games. It was more fun to go to Rockers games than it was to Cavaliers games. And I think that's just how far it had gone, and had dropped in interest."

The few thousand or so fans who did show up for games couldn't care less about the Cavs. They were there to see the opponents, whether it was Kobe and the Lakers, Allen Iverson and the Sixers, or Kevin Garnett and the Timberwolves. Remarkably, that unfortunate truth dates back to the Cavaliers' days at the Coliseum, even the successful times.

"When Michael [Jordan] would come to town," Karlovec continued, "you'd see all this red and black, or even in the late '80s and early '90s, Boston would come to town with [Larry] Bird, and you'd see all these green coats in the stands. So from that standpoint, to me, having 20,000 people there to see, say, the Lakers, they weren't there to support our team. They would root for the Cavaliers, but they were there to see the Lakers."

"It used to tick me off," said Gordon Gund. "I couldn't believe that, that people would not support their own team! That's how deep the difficulty was that we inherited when we bought the team in 1983. The franchise had really been badly handled before that."

THE ARENA WAS ROCKING

The events of May 22, 2003, completely changed Cavaliers basketball, gave it a new identity—or rather, gave it *an* identity. The Cavs won the NBA Draft Lottery that evening, granting them the number-one pick in the college player pool—in other words, LeBron James. Fans could not buy tickets fast enough. Sixteen home games sold out, compared to two the year before. It was incredible.

SHOWTIME (LeBron Style)

THE CAVALIERS SAW AN ATTENDANCE BOOM AT HOME IN 2003-04 AS THEY AVERAGED 18,288 FANS PER GAME, UP 6,791 FROM 2002-03 WHEN THEY RANKED LAST IN THE LEAGUE. THE 59 PERCENT INCREASE RANKS AS THE LARGEST SEASON-TO-SEASON INCREASE IN NBA HISTORY (WITH BOTH SEASONS PLAYED IN THE SAME FACILITY). THE CAVS HAD 16 SELLOUTS AS OPPOSED TO JUST TWO IN '02-'03. THE TEAM WAS MORE OF AN ATTRACTION ON THE ROAD, AS WELL, AVERAGING 18,755—SECOND IN THE LEAGUE—UP NEARLY 3,000 FROM THE YEAR BEFORE. THE CAVALIERS SOLD OUT 33 ROAD GAMES AS OPPOSED TO SIX THE PREVIOUS SEASON.

"Basketball is fun in Cleveland again," said Bob Karlovec. "There was an excitement around Gund Arena last year that had not been around the Cavaliers since the Price-Daugherty-Nance days."

Joe Tait said it was a simple matter of seats filled with fans as opposed to seats filled with air. He added that, as the season unfolded and the "LeBron" novelty wore off, the real basketball fans took center stage.

"And, fortunately," he said, "they held the fort in pretty good numbers. The reponse of the crowd has certainly been the best that we have had down there maybe in the history of the Cavaliers at Gund Arena."

"The crowds near the end of the year that were on their feet screaming for the Cavaliers to win games," Chad Estis said, "were so different than early on when people wanted to get into the Gund just to see 'The Kid.'"

Bruce Drennan agreed wholeheartedly but put a different spin on it.

"It's a younger crowd down there," he said. "It's date night to go see LeBron. It's an ego thing. People get into, 'Oh, I've got my tickets, I've got my season tickets, I've got my package, my seats are here, my seats are there.' You never had that at Gund Arena since the Cavs moved there. Just the attitude of the fans, the atmosphere, the electricity…that wasn't there before LeBron's arrival. Everybody's into it. That's the thing. The whole community bands together with something like this."

Drennan commended the Cavaliers' marketing efforts in keeping fans entertained.

"I think they put on a good show," he said. "It was a fun event to go to, where before it wasn't fun to go to a Cavs game. It's still outrageously priced, but you don't mind now because it's such a fun event."

THE JAKE'S CADDY NO MORE

Jeff Sack recalled the days in the mid- to late 1990s when the Cavaliers struggled, while the Indians, their neighbors at Jacobs Field, enjoyed so much success that they sold out 455 straight home games.

"We used to joke," recalled Sack, "that people thought Gund Arena was a storage building for where the Indians kept their bats and playing equipment. And here, this [Cavaliers] organization has literally turned into the toast of Cleveland."

TALK, TALK, TALK

The world of sports talk radio took a dramatic turn when the Cavaliers secured the number-one pick in the 2003 draft. Prior to the lottery, hosts all over town found it practically impossible to coax listeners into calling in and talking Cavs basketball. It was like trying to squeeze water from a stone. But after the lottery, LeBron James and Cavaliers basketball were all that sports talk radio callers cared about.

"Words can't even explain the difference," Kenny Roda said, adding that the increase in calls actually began as the 2002-03 season unfolded and the Cavaliers were positioning themselves for a high draft pick.

"It was LeBron," Mike Snyder said of his Cavaliers post-game call-in show, "who got me through that season the year before in a sense. When the Cavs would lose, we would talk about LeBron and, even when they lost, it wasn't a bad thing because it was maybe one more ping-pong ball."

"We barely took any calls before," added Roda. "Once they did get LeBron James, even during baseball and football seasons, the callers wanted to talk LeBron James. And then once the season started on opening night in Sacramento, and with the numbers he put up on national TV, people started seeing what I saw three years ago."

"I could blackmail the callers with tickets," Bruce Drennan said, "and they wouldn't talk about the Cavs. Now it's, arguably, next to the Browns, the hottest topic."

It was no different for Snyder.

"I took more calls last year," he said, "than probably the three previous years combined."

It's a Cav, No Bull

Everywhere you looked during the Cavaliers' 2003–04 season, you saw number 23 jerseys. They were wine and gold, though, not red and black. For years, Chicago Bulls superstar Michael Jordan was *the* number 23. Times have changed. Jordan is living the charmed life of retirement. Now, LeBron James is number 23.

"To see the arena with so many young kids, especially," Gund said, "who were wearing LeBron James jerseys was remarkable."

The number 23 jersey wasn't seen solely at Gund Arena. It was spotted at other locales in the Cleveland area—at the malls, on the streets, and espicially at rec centers.

"I coach my son's basketball and baseball teams," said Kenny Roda, "and the kids look up to LeBron so much already. The number of "23" jerseys I'd see at a basketball practice or in a rec center…it's phenomenal. You go in there and there's the home, there's the away, version of it. There are LeBron jerseys everywhere.

"So having gone into a rec center the year before and not seeing any Cavalier jerseys, and then going in this year and seeing two out of every three kids having a Cavalier jersey on, that's the impact he's had off the court. And they're not only kids on my team but even teenagers, girls too. Hispanic, African-American, white kids—he appeals to everybody."

Perhaps the most astonishing location they were spotted was in opposing NBA arenas.

"There was wine all over the place," said Gordon Gund, "in Philadelphia, in New York, up in Boston. It was really remarkable."

HE'S STILL THE MOTOR

Sellout crowds. LeBron paraphernalia everywhere. The wine and gold was back. Charged-up climate at the Gund. Cavalier Fever was running rampant as the 2003-04 season progressed. But according to Terry Pluto, although all of that is fine and dandy, the bottom line is still LeBron James. Period.

"It's kind of like, you could take a race car," Pluto said, "and paint it all up as beautiful as you like with a great stereo system, etc. If you don't have the motor, nobody cares about it. LeBron's the motor. You've got no motor, you've got just a nice-looking car sitting in the parking lot, and nobody's paying any attention to it."

CHANGE OF TUNE

There were many Northeast Ohioans, according to Terry Pluto, who thought it was inappropriate for LeBron James to be attending a catholic school. They felt it was wrong for James and his Akron St. Vincent-St. Mary teammates to be globe-trotting all over the country.

"But the moment he became a Cavalier," Pluto said, "all of a sudden there were no criticisms of LeBron. It was like, 'Boy, our native son is now going to represent us on the national stage.'"

TGIM (Thank God It's Monday)

Austin Carr has been a television analyst for Cavaliers games since the 1998-99 season. The last time the team qualified for the playoffs was the year before.

Not the best timing in the world.

In fact, in Carr's first five seasons on the job, the Cavs' winning percentage dropped each year, from a respectable .440 to a paltry .207. Carr admitted it was difficult keeping a positive attitude on the air through those troubled times, especially in the harrowing 2002-03 season that produced just 17 wins.

"You'd try to look for positive things," he said, "but there was just nothing there. So what you'd end up doing was, sometimes, you'd start getting a little too negative but, at the same time, that's all that was on the floor."

And Carr tells it like it is. Covering the Cavs is just more fun when the team is winning.

Opponents on LeBron

"He's unbelievable, incredible really. If he continues to work hard and stay hungry, it could be ugly. The poise that he has on the basketball court...he has that swagger, nothing rattles him at all. He's got extremely high confidence and he's a real competitor. At the age of 19, that's scary. He's a hell of a player, and I enjoyed watching him play."

—*Tracy McGrady,* Orlando Magic

"It was tough," he said. "You enjoy your work because of what it is, for what you do but, at the same time, you know that there was no hope there. Once the hope comes, not only do you enjoy your job, but you love your job, because there's potential for success there."

In 2003-04, the hope came, as well as the potential for success—mainly because of one LeBron James. The Cavaliers more than doubled their win total from the previous season, finishing 35-47 and coming within a whisker of the playoffs.

"You started having more positive things happen on the floor," Carr continued, "and it became a lot easier to do the games because it was all positive stuff. You didn't have to try to dress anything up because everything out there was good. Now, granted, they went through some negative stretches but, at the same time ... you don't get weighed down with all negative stuff. You definitely have a little bit more adrenaline flowing now than in the past."

SALES THE EZ WAY

As outer market event specialist for the Cavaliers, Campy Russell speaks to organizations such as civic groups and business groups, aiming to promote interest in the team. Most of Russell's attention is focused in and around Akron, Canton, Youngstown, and Columbus. Russell said that prior to LeBron James's arrival, it was difficult to convince people to buy tickets.

"It was a tough sell," admitted Russell, a Cavaliers forward from 1974-79, "and not necessarily just from the outer market area but, period."

Provide fans with a poor product, and even the best salesman in the world would have a hard time.

"We were coming off a very bad season," Russell said, "and it didn't look like we were going in any kind of direction. One of the things I kept hearing over and over was, 'I bought these tickets with the thought of sharing them with my customers' or doing those types of things. Their whole thread was, 'I can't even *give* the tickets away' because people were just not interested due to the level of play."

When LeBron came aboard, Russell's job suddenly became easier and more enjoyable. The difference was like night and day.

"You hear the old adage a lot," Russell said, "'What a difference a day makes, or a week makes, or a year makes.' Truly, it was that. And now, since [LeBron's] here, and we've turned this thing around, those same people are calling *us* and inquiring about the opportunities to purchase tickets."

In Awe

Gordon Gund has been in the sports business for nearly 30 years. He has never experienced a turnaround, or a change in attitude, of a marketplace like what happened in 2003-04 with the Cavaliers. He is just thrilled for the Cleveland fans, whom he called the best sports fans in the world.

"I'm very glad," he said, "now that they have a team that is very much theirs because the superstar—or potential superstar—on the team is right from the marketplace. I think there are a lot of great, and very exciting, things to come."

IT'S STILL CLEVELAND

Ever since the Cavaliers won the 2003 NBA Draft Lottery and the right to draft LeBron James, the perception of the team changed. National television appearances. LeBron and Cavaliers merchandise everywhere. Capacity crowds at home and on the road. But according to Terry Pluto, the scope of Cleveland remained the same.

"I don't think a winning player, or winning team," Pluto said, "changes the way an area, or a team, is looked at in the nation. I just don't buy that. Yes, it's nice that the team gets on TV more, and they say more nice things about Cleveland, and so on. But Cleveland is still Cleveland, Boston's Boston, Gary, Indiana's Gary, Indiana. I think we, in sports, sometimes want it to be that way, just a little sense of self-importance.

"Now, for the people living here, it's more of a conversation thing, it becomes something to do at night, to check the games out, to follow the team, to second guess the coach. That's where it has more of an impact. Nationally, okay, fine, so Charles Barkley's now saying nice things about the Cavaliers instead of bad things but, in retrospect, so what? If you live in Cleveland, you do it for a reason. Maybe you don't want to spend 600 bucks a month to park your car in New York. So there."

Chapter 8

STANDING "O" FOR THE WINE AND GOLD

AT LEAST WE LOOK GOOD

For the better part of their first 13 seasons, the Cleveland Cavaliers were a mockery. Other than a few years in the mid- to late 1970s, the team was the butt of many jokes because it lost—and lost a lot. The losing was punctuated by a pair of 15-win seasons, one coming in the Cavs' expansion year of 1970-71, the other in 1981–82, the second of three seasons in which the team was owned by Ted Stepien. Stepien nearly drove the franchise to ruin by running the team so ineptly, making so many ludicrous trades that the NBA actually banned the Cavaliers from any more deals. Stepien was so out of control, he made former Cleveland Indians general manager Frank "Trader" Lane seem like Mr. Conservative.

There was one consistent plus with the Cavaliers during this time period—their team colors. Although the Cavs donned three different styles, the colors remained the same—wine and gold. They were captivating colors, appealing, unique. The Cavaliers not only *wore* the wine and gold, they *were* the wine and gold. That was their hallmark, as longtime Cavs radio play-by-play announcer Joe Tait would bellow after a fine Cavaliers rally: "A standing 'O' for the guys in gold!"

The team logo utilized the words "Cleveland Cavaliers" emblazoned around a basketball, and featured the silhouette of a Cavalier figure thrusting a sword. The logo, along with the colors, was not only apropos but attractive as well.

PAJAMA PARTY

Gordon Gund and his brother, George, purchased the Cavaliers from Stepien in 1983. The Gunds aimed to alleviate the stench still lingering from the Stepien era. They overhauled the team colors lock, stock, and barrel from the traditional wine and gold to a burnt orange, white and royal blue. They scrapped the team logo, substituting the word "CAVS," with a net forming the "V." By doing so, the Gund brothers took the team's most recognizable symbol and tossed it into some cow pasture in Richfield. The new "CAVS" logo was designed so fans would no longer think of the team as the "Cavaliers." The team would be reincarnated as the "Cavs."

The decision to alter the team's identity was an unpopular one to say the least. Colors and logos are crucial. They are key factors in how fans connect to a team. Players and coaches come and go. Colors and logos ought to stay the same. Cavs ownership failed to follow that unwritten rule. And although the team provided fans with some fine basketball throughout the next two decades, that important bond was broken.

"I think the area identified with the [wine and gold]," said Campy Russell, "to the point that it's almost like sacrilege."

The Cavaliers instituted several changes in their uniform. Color combinations included various shades of blue, black, and back to orange. Some colors were splashed, or swooshed, across the jersey and/or shorts. Eventually, the team adopted a logo featuring a basketball arching into a stylized net, positioned above the word "CAVS."

Who were these guys? Where was that majestic combination of wine and gold?

IT'S THE CAVALIERS AGAIN

At long last, after extensive research that encompassed hundreds of videotaped interviews with fans throughout the Cleveland area, plus an Internet survey (a first for the NBA) that elicited 12,000 responses, the Cavaliers organization decided it was time.

The wine and gold was coming back.

"It became quite clear to us," Gordon Gund said, "that wine and gold was what people in our marketplace felt really represented the Cavs, those two colors. We concluded if that's what our marketplace wanted, we wanted to make sure that's what we had."

---

500 PERCENT?
IS THERE SUCH A FIGURE?

MERCHANDISE SALES IN THE CAVALIERS TEAM SHOP, ON CLEVELANDCAVALIERS.COM, AND IN-ARENA DURING GAMES INCREASED 500 PERCENT IN 2003-04 FROM THE PREVIOUS SEASON.

Russell compared the circumstances to an athletic endeav-or of which fans in that region of the country are well aware—football.

"Even when the Browns went to Baltimore," he explained, "there couldn't have been another team brought in here with-out it being orange and brown, it couldn't have happened. And taking it a little further, it's almost like taking away the maize-and-blue of Michigan, or the scarlet-and-gray of Ohio State, because they're all connected to that, and I think that's how fans looked at it."

Said David Kelly, "I had been calling for a return to the wine and gold for years, much like a lot of people. That's the history, and that was a time when you hearkened on the Miracle in Richfield. That was the finest time of the franchise history."

"[Former WKNR personality] Kendall [Lewis] and I lob-bied for that for years," Greg Brinda added. "And to be hon-est with you, I think we were two of the people who really pushed for it. We baited them, we goaded them, we demand-ed, and we finally got it. We were the ones who were vocally pushing for this for years."

On October 9, 2002, when LeBron James was merely a pipedream in the minds of Cavs fans, "a new expression of wine and gold" was unveiled as the official team colors but would not be utilized, however, until the 2003–04 season. That made for a timely twist of fate.

"It was fortunate," recalled Gund, "that the actual uniforms were first introduced just a couple of weeks before the lottery. I think the colors, along with LeBron, along with what we've done in terms of adding new life to our management, makes for a very exciting confluence of events that all came togeth-er. We were, therefore, able to do a much better job of making the most out of the opportunity we got in the lottery."

The primary colors are a crimson-hued wine and a metal-lic gold. While they represent updated versions of the

Cavaliers' original colors, the new colors are both contempo-
rary and timeless. Dark blue also is used as an accent color on
the new logo and uniforms. The use of blue is in recognition
of the Cavaliers teams of the 1990s. Furthermore, "Cavaliers,"
not "Cavs," is inscribed across the front of the home jerseys.
That was not by accident.

"We wanted to return," Komoroski said, "to being known
as the 'Cavaliers'—'A daring team of fearless young men who
were always willing to fight, no matter what the odds.' I mean,
that's, in essence, the Cavaliers. It's a positive, a swashbuckling
Cavalier."

Komoroski went on to talk of the strength and passion of
the Cleveland sports market, its appreciation for history, and
the heritage of the Cavs, and how significant the changeover
to the new expression of wine and gold is to the marketplace.

"It was just a phenomenal, if you want to say, halo, of everything that's taken place," he said. "We have yet to get one com-
ment from any fan to say, 'Change back to the old colors.'"

"Now you bring back a lot of the fans," said Austin Carr,
"who were borderline fans because of the feeling they had for
the wine and gold."

"People were tired of this blue stuff," Brinda added, "and
they were ready for the history and the tradition."

Kelly expanded on that thought.

"The new colors are just different," he said. "They make for
a different shade from any other team. Everybody has blue and
everybody has black in their uniforms, but wine and gold was
something that was Cleveland."

"It kind of closed the circle," Russell said, "because there
was a big disconnection."

JUST WIN, BABY

Some fans have no concern whatsoever regarding the shade, or style, of uniforms athletes wear. Winning is the most important thing.

"When the Cavs were winning 57 games," said Larry Pantages, "and wearing powder blue, and a little bit of orange trim, and white, nobody cared. The Seinfeld line of 'You cheer for the uniforms'…there's some truth to that."

OPPONENTS ON LEBRON

"HE'S A GREAT PLAYER AND HE'S LEBRON JAMES. HE'S ALREADY ONE OF THE BEST PLAYERS IN THE LEAGUE. YOU'RE IMPRESSED WITH HIS SKILLS AND HIS BODY. I THINK HE PLAYS WITH A DEMEANOR AND A SENSE OF THE GAME THAT'S WAY, WAY BEYOND HIS YEARS. HE DESERVES A LOT OF CREDIT. THERE'S A LOT GOING ON IN HIS LIFE, WITH ALL THIS HOOPLA AND EVERYTHING, AND HE'S ABLE TO FOCUS ON THE GAME AND JUST TRY TO GET BETTER."

——*Gregg Popovich*, San Antonio Spurs head coach

Chapter 9

LeBron.
The Miracle.
The Comparisons.

Berserk in the Bicentennial

Long before LeBron James was even thought of—when his mother was still in grade school—there was a basketball explosion in Northeast Ohio that was quite possibly more thrilling than even James and the Cavaliers' 2003-04 season. It occurred in the spring of 1976 and was dubbed the "Miracle in Richfield," a 36-day stretch from mid-April to mid-May in which basketball fans in Northeast Ohio were delirious over the Cavaliers. Cavs fever was rampant. Five years removed from their expansion season of 1970-71, the Cavaliers qualified for their first ever playoff berth. They stunned the favored Washington Bullets in an awesome seven-game series punctuated by three miracle Cavs conquests.

"I've never seen a crowd, night after night, act like they did," former *Plain Dealer* sportswriter Bill Nichols recalled. "It was just complete euphoria. It was the wildest, the most exciting, time I ever had in 30 years as a sportswriter."

Center Jim Chones broke his right foot in a practice session prior to the Eastern Conference Championship series against the hallowed, but beatable, Boston Celtics. With Akron native Nate Thurmond pressed into more minutes than his 36-year-old body could withstand, the Cavaliers took the Celtics six games before wilting.

"During a lot of those playoff games," longtime *Plain Dealer* sportswriter Bob Dolgan said, "fans would show up an hour before the game and chant, 'Bring on the Cavs! Bring on the Cavs! Bring on the Cavs!' One time, [Cavs head coach] Bill Fitch was trying to talk to one of his players in the locker room. The noise was so loud that it caused a chalkboard in there to fall down! Because it took so long to get out of the Coliseum parking lot, fans would sit up in one of the bars upstairs until it cleared out a little. They'd show replays of the games on the TVs in there, and the fans would be yelling and screaming at the replays!"

The sensation that entire season, especially in the playoffs, might go down as the most exhilarating stretch in Cleveland sports annals. How does the LeBron-led Cavaliers' 2003-04 season compare with the events of some 30 years beforehand? Was the excitement level greater? Lesser? Equal?

NOT EVEN CLOSE

"The folks down at the Gund," Joe Tait said, "have not even come close to what we had out at the Coliseum in the 'Miracle in Richfield'. I mean, they're doing well, they're doing better than I thought they probably ever would. But, by the same token, that 'Miracle in Richfield' year, the audience, the fan reaction, it was unbelievable.

"You just have to hope that maybe, as LeBron gets better, the fans will rise to the occasion and some day I can tell you,

'Yeah, it's just like it was back at the Coliseum in '76.' I think if the Cavs head for a championship, if they're playing in the championship round, you may well see excitement at the same level because then they would have taken winning to the highest level we've ever seen with the Cavaliers."

Bill Nichols was there firsthand in 1976. He admitted his take might be a tad biased since he has fallen off the radar screen since his retirement more than a decade ago.

"I thought it was more exciting then," Nichols said. "You had moments with LeBron's first year, but I think the euphoria of those '76 playoffs was just something I know I'll never see again, and I don't know who will in this town. I think this could maybe reach it if they get into title contention, deep into the playoffs, and LeBron would be a leader."

Bob Dolgan agreed. He doubts if the Miracle season will ever be duplicated.

"The Coliseum was fairly new," he said. "The team had been pretty lousy. All of those people were so anxious. It just became a phenomenon. If the Cavaliers win a conference title and are playing for an NBA Championship, that might outdo it."

"The excitement last season," Greg Brinda added, "was not even close to the excitement during the 'Miracle in Richfield'

FOREIGN AFFAIR

Media members from 21 different countries were issued 137 credentials to cover the Cavaliers in 2003-04. Nine countries visited the Cavs at home, and 12 countries covered the team on the road.

season. It was just way, way over the top that season. This was nice, but this was nothing compared to that."

"There is no comparison between the 2003-04 season and the 'Miracle in Richfield' season," Hal Lebovitz said. "That season was something special. They had a chance to win a championship, the '03-'04 team didn't."

SHINING MOMENTS TO BEHOLD

When the Cavaliers won the NBA Draft Lottery on Thursday evening, May 22, 2003, Cavs fans all over town were ecstatic. It was quite possibly the most exciting single moment in franchise history, and it didn't even happen on the basketball court!

The only other instance in team annals that rivals the sheer joy of that night was what occurred on another Thursday, nearly 30 years before, on April 29, 1976, the summit of the "Miracle in Richfield." This one occurred on the court, however, at the old Coliseum in front of a then-NBA record playoff crowd of 21,564. The Cavaliers, just six years old and in their first postseason, had a precarious 87-85 lead over the Washington Bullets in the seventh and deciding game of an Eastern Conference semifinal series. Moments earlier, Cavs guard Dick Snyder had driven to the hoop and banked in a running, one-handed shot from five feet away with four seconds left to give the Cavs the lead.

After a Bullets' time out, Washington's Wes Unseld lobbed the ball toward the Bullets' basket. Snyder knocked the ball free. Phil Chenier picked it up in the right corner and threw up a 20-foot shot that missed. Fans rushed the floor. One of the baskets was torn down. It was almost like a college atmosphere. It was euphoria. The Cavaliers, the darlings of Cleveland, were on their way to play the mighty Boston Celtics for the Eastern Conference Championship.

"I think," Mike Snyder said, "the joy of the moment the Cavaliers won the lottery to the joy of the moment when the Cavs beat Washington in Game 7 in the 1976 playoffs is comparable. I was there when they beat the Bullets that night, and that was just phenomenal."

"Those are two experiences," said Austin Carr, "that I will never forget even though they were on different ends of the spectrum, and one had nothing to do with a game. But the excitement that was in Champps at our lottery party that night was just as rabid and similar and exciting as it was when we beat Washington in that seventh game, that's exactly what it was like."

OPPONENTS ON LEBRON

"HE IS A PHENOMENAL YOUNG PLAYER. IT'S UNCANNY FOR A YOUNG PLAYER TO PLAY THAT WAY. HE PLAYS LIKE HE'S BEEN AROUND A LONG TIME, AND HE'S JUST IN THE DOOR. HE CERTAINLY WILL GET BETTER AS HIS CAREER PROGRESSES. HE'S VERY POISED, VERY POLISHED, VERY CONFIDENT, AND THEY HAVE A VERY, VERY GOOD BASKETBALL PLAYER IN LEBRON JAMES. THERE'S NO QUESTION ABOUT THAT."

—*Johnny Davis*, Orlando Magic head coach

BOTH WERE SPECIAL

If the "Miracle in Richfield" was a momentous event, one that any longtime Cavaliers fan will never forget, then the rookie season of LeBron James was unforgettable as well. They both have their niche in Cleveland Cavaliers history.

"I would call last year a sense of anticipation about what's to come," Larry Pantages said, "and I would call the 'Miracle' year a sense of, 'We're in the moment now, we made the play-offs and—oh, my gosh—in the first series we ever played in, it goes seven games and we win with a Dick Snyder shot, and then we go to the Celtics and a chance to go to the finals and Chones breaks his foot.' You saw Phoenix coming out of the West, and they seemed like a beatable team.

"They both ['75-76 and '02-03 Cavaliers] had their own character, but the '76 experience was a time the Indians were down, the Browns were down…Cleveland fans were hungry for something and, boy, when these guys won 49 games in the regular season, it was like, 'Wow!' The 'Miracle' year had its own special place, and LeBron has his own place, and thank God the next generation of fans here can read about the old stuff and now live the moment of the new stuff."

Chapter 10

KING JAMES

LIGHTING IT UP INDEED

When LeBron James was asked by a member of the media after the 2003 NBA Draft Lottery if he was disappointed he was not going to a major market like New York, or Chicago, or L.A. LeBron replied with a prediction: "Ya'll come to Cleveland. It'll be lit up like Vegas."

LeBron was wrong. He lit it up like Vegas on New Year's Eve! A Cavaliers game in 2003-04 was undoubtedly a different experience than in recent years. Gund Arena was rocking. The atmosphere was electric. It was a whole new world for the Cleveland Cavaliers, a world they could easily get used to.

LATE-NIGHT LOITERING

Fans would do just about anything to get a piece of LeBron James. Thousands throughout the season waited—sometimes in polar temperatures at all hours of the night—outside hotels in NBA cities across the country waiting to get a glimpse, take a picture of, cop an autograph, from the young star.

"You sit there," said Joe Tait, "and you wonder, 'Don't these people have a life?' I mean, they're out there at three o'clock in the morning in the rain and snow but, at three o'clock in the morning, who can blame [LeBron] if he heads inside?"

"It was madness," Ira Newble recalled. "Everywhere we went, whether we got in at six o'clock in the evening or sometimes three and four in the morning, it was just amazing the attention that 'LB' brought. If it was a kid, LeBron would sign [an autograph]. If it was an adult, he usually wouldn't sign it. If he did that, he would be signing all day long plus, not to mention, a lot of people get stuff and sell it on Ebay, so you can't just sign everybody's autograph."

"I don't know how they know when we get to where we're going," said Mark Osowski, "but they're always there."

"It's mostly people taking pictures of I don't know what," Terry Pluto added, "because usually you're shooting a picture of the bald head in front of you. So that's there, but a lot of that was even going on when he was at St. Vincent."

Jim Paxson recalled the Cavaliers' stop in Portland on the last leg of their season-opening road trip when there was a crowd waiting at the Cavs' hotel.

"There were 50-75 people walled up," Paxson said. "LeBron came through, and everybody was screaming his name. There was one old-timer who's been there since I played there in '79, and probably longer than that, who was trying to get autographs, and trying to give directions, announcing, 'Now, if we want to get LeBron to sign these things, let's all be civil, and be nice to him!'"

After a game against the Timberwolves in Minnesota, Chad Estis saw something that blew his mind away. He was standing by the team bus waiting to go to the airport to fly back to Cleveland.

"[Minnesota Vikings star receiver] Randy Moss and a friend of his are waiting for LeBron to come out," Estis recalled. "So he came out with a pair of his shoes autographed, and gave them to Randy. LeBron was only there for about 30 seconds, and we were gone. What amazed me was that Randy looked as if he was a fan who had just met his idol and received a pair of autographed shoes!

"A 19-year-old kid to be in a position where he's giving an autographed item to someone like Randy Moss, and they're that enthused about it, was a little bit shocking."

JUST MENTION HIS NAME AND...

When Mike Snyder conducted his Cavaliers postgame show and LeBron was the guest, all hell would break loose.

"I would say, 'Let's hear from LeBron,'" Snyder said, "and I'd immediately have a crowd of people run over to the table and say, 'Is LeBron gonna be here?'"

It was like mice running to cheese.

"Where I do the show is where the players walk out," Snyder said, "and every night there's just a mob waiting for LeBron. And every night he signs a bunch of autographs on his way out the door, usually for kids. But if you just mention his name, automatically you have people come over and say, 'Is LeBron gonna be here, is LeBron gonna be here?'"

HOT TICKET OUT OF TOWN

The Cavaliers sold out 33 road games in 2003-04, compared to six the previous season. They were the feature attraction on other NBA teams' ticket packages before the season. That's what happens when you have a superstar the magnitude of LeBron James on your roster.

"Teams traditionally package partial plans, or mini-plans, 10-game plans, five-game plans," explained Chad Estis, "and they'll use the more attractive teams in the NBA as the lead game. For example, you have the Lakers in a plan, and then you might have some teams that aren't as attractive to help along with that plan, and the Lakers will sell the plan. Well, every team in the NBA was using the Cleveland Cavaliers as one of their lead games. I mean, we had always been the throw-in game—you know, *with* the Lakers. During September and October when those plans were being formulated, I've got friends of mine from other teams who called me, saying, 'Your game is our lead game in the plan!' It was just a total 100 percent flip from the year before."

Bob Karlovec saw it firsthand all the way out on the West Coast. Karlovec was in San Francisco in September 2003 covering a Cleveland Browns game against the 49ers.

"I happened to see an advertising pamphlet for the Golden State Warriors," he recalled, "and they had LeBron featured prominently on it. So they were pushing him, promoting him, almost as much as he was being promoted in his home city. In some cities, depending on how good or bad the teams were, that might be one of the few games they would sell out. It was almost like Michael Jordan coming to Cleveland to get their 20,000 for Jordan being there. Golden State got a sellout because LeBron came in."

LIVING LEGEND

Granted, there was no CNN, no ESPN, no Internet, 30 or 40 years ago. It is still a safe bet, however, that LeBron James is the most coveted, publicized individual in the history of Cleveland sports.

"LeBron James is an international figure now," Bill Livingston said. "Nobody in a mainstream sport has ever had this kind of hype. I mean, golf is not basketball. The only thing I can think of that would be similar was if Bob Feller had done what he did in our era. He would have been as big as LeBron because he struck out 17 big league batters when he was 17 years old and then went back to high school!"

"I don't think there's any question," added Mike Snyder, "that this is the one star magnitude player that we've had probably since...I have to go back to Jim Brown to compare anybody else who has had not only that impact on the field but also off the field."

Bill Nichols concurred. He brought up even more Cleveland sports legends that LeBron is leaving in the dust.

"I'm thinking back to Rocky Colavito," he said, "and even way back to the '48 Indians. There's never been anybody who hit this town like LeBron James. He's an incredible young man. Not even Rocky, and they had a big phrase: 'Don't knock the Rock.' But not to the effect that it was on this kid. I couldn't believe it, I just couldn't believe the excitement around this young man.

Nichols continued, "I go back to the first year of the Browns with Otto Graham and those people, and it wasn't like this either. And Bernie Kosar being released, that had a sour taste for, I think, every Browns fan in town. He was much beloved as an athlete here, and he was a good athlete, a good quarterback, not a great one, but a good one. And they had some exciting times with Bernie and, prior to that, with Brian Sipe. But nothing like LeBron."

On top of all of that, James emanates from Cleveland's back yard—Akron, just a short spin down Interstate 77.

"You're talking about a kid who played 35 miles away in high school," said Rick Noland, "and he's got an entire city there following him. There's been nothing even close that I can think of."

LeBron James's winning smile has earned him a lot of fans. (AP/WWP)

"It's a hometown guy getting to play in his home town as a pro," Larry Pantages said. "It's a great story, and the story has a potential to be even greater. I mean, sports is on page A1 in the *Akron Beacon Journal* a lot, and it's because of stories like this, like when Tiger Woods comes to town. LeBron has a wide audience and a lot of popularity."

Stars Are Out

A number of celebrities from the motion picture, television, and music industries were spotted at Cavaliers games in 2003-04. At times, it seemed like the Staples Center in Los Angeles.

"We had Geraldo come in for a night," Len Komoroski recalled. "Tara Reid came to a game. And the great thing about Geraldo and Tara Reid was, coming to the Midwest, they could have a little more fun with themselves. Tara participated in an on-court promotion where she was actually throwing a football, and somebody was catching it with her. Geraldo actually took place in a conga line on the floor."

Media Madhouse
We Have a Few Questions

Media types from all over the world descended on the Cavaliers in 2003-04 to cover LeBron James. Nine countries were represented at home games, a dozen at road games. Locally, the coverage increased, too. It was truly a sight to see.

"The first time I met LeBron," Paul Silas said, "was at Gund Arena soon after the draft. There must've been about 100 reporters there, and I just said, 'Oh my God, is this the way it's going to be all season long?'"

Media access to the young superstar, though, was limited—for a reason. For instance, the Cavaliers' public relations personnel proposed the idea of allowing James to have a podium before and after games. Paul Silas wanted no part of that.

"I didn't want it to be a total difference in him and the rest of the team," Silas said. "I think that's what made it work. You can't treat your players differently. LeBron would not have wanted that, either. I think I allowed it the first home game because there were so many reporters there. But after that he was just like anybody else. At road games, after he would go out and do his pregame warmup, they were allowed to come in and have five minutes or so with him and that was it. You have to do it that way because the most important thing is winning and LeBron playing well. Certainly you have to be aware of it and accommodate as much as possible, but the bottom line is he has to prepare himself for the game."

"Nobody ever had a real one on one with LeBron," said Bill Livingston. "I think *Sports Illustrated* had 22 minutes, and 12 of that was the photographs. [*SI's*] Jack McCallum only had 10 minutes with him. It's kind of like Tiger Woods, just not as shielded."

Lowe's, Beware!

Even the media resorted to unusual tactics in order to access LeBron James. Photographers, for instance, began staking out stepladders and guarding them as closely as a mother cat protects her newborn kittens—to ensure they would get a shot of LeBron over the media throng in front of them.

"This became the norm throughout the year," Len Komoroski said. "The premium market for stepladders became huge."

SAVE IT

LeBron James memorabilia sold like hotcakes during the 2003–04 season, and rightfully so. Kenny Roda was one individual who was buying—and thinking—big.

"In the collectors business," Roda said, "the rookie year is always the biggest because it is all of the 'firsts.' I have a box score from his first game, his rookie basketball, too. I went out and bought a pair of size 15 LeBron James shoes, the first shoes LeBron ever had out, because I remember hearing what the first Air Jordans went for later in his career; over in Japan, you could sell them for $3,500. So I went out and spent the 110 bucks for a pair of LeBron James shoes that I'm not going to wear. I can't wear them. I wear a size 10. But I went out and bought them because I think he's going to be something special."

The Cavaliers donated a LeBron-signed jersey that sold for $4,500 at a charity function.

"That was phenomenal," said Chad Estis. "I think that's unheard of for autographed jerseys in sports at a charitable function."

LeBron-a-licious

Apparently, a professional athlete does not have to play for a New York, Los Angeles, or Chicago team to cash in on endorsement deals. At least not if your name is LeBron James.

"Athletes would not come here as free agents before," said Kenny Roda, "because they couldn't cash in as far as marketability. They couldn't get endorsements. Well, by getting LeBron James in Cleveland, that just blew that small-market, mid-market stuff totally out of the water.

"LeBron James is now Nike's highest-paid athlete. He is to Powerade what Michael Jordan was to Gatorade. He's endorsing Sprite, that whole Coca-Cola family, he's endorsing video games, Upper Deck, Juice Batteries. He's got his own bubble gum coming out. They're creating a LeBron flavor, his own special flavor of bubble gum! It proves that if you're good enough, regardless of the market you're in, you'll be able to cash in on endorsements."

PEERLESS PUBLICITY

The enormous volume of publicity that LeBron James attracted to the city of Cleveland was priceless. It was at no cost, as well.

"There's no Chamber of Commerce campaign," Len Komoroski said, "that we could have enacted in Northeast Ohio that could've replicated the type of attention that was drawn to our marketplace."

"Getting LeBron James just put Cleveland on the map," said Kenny Roda. "Every time you see him now, you think of the Cleveland Cavaliers."

LEBRON EQUALS RATINGS

The television networks and cable channels couldn't get enough of LeBron James in 2003-04. The Cavaliers were on national TV 16 times, more than the prior 10 seasons combined.

"I posed this question," Len Komoroski said, "to some media members at one point during the season: 'When's the last time we've had a Cleveland team that's actually been desired by the networks?' They said, 'Never.' I mean, we've had teams certainly of major regional interest, but we have fans in Boise, Idaho, now who have never been to a game, and have never been to Cleveland for that matter, because they've now jumped on the Cavaliers bandwagon."

HAVEN'T WE HEARD THIS BEFORE?

There was such a large number of media members from around the world coming and going, covering the Cavaliers throughout the season, that Paul Silas and some of the players were answering the same questions halfway through the year. They handled it gamely, though.

"They knew that just because they had heard the question 40 times before," Rick Noland said, "that was that person's first chance to ask it, so they still did it. Eventually, it kind of wore them down, and you could almost see them become robots."

ROAD LESS TRAVELED

There had been a growing apathy surrounding the Cleveland Cavaliers in the years leading up to the 2003-04 campaign. And clearly the team was not on the national forefront as it is now. With that in mind, and with a young man by the name of LeBron James on the way, the organization took a step back and assessed the situation.

"It would have been a very obvious thing," Cavaliers vice president of marketing Tracy Marek said, "to plaster LeBron all over everything. So we actually chose not to do that, and I think that if you look at what the team did, it was a very purposeful step forward but had little to do with LeBron.

"It's easy for the rest of the world to take this one individual—who is deserving—and put him on a pedestal of sorts, and that's fine. But in our mind, he was still somebody in our organization who needed to be fostered, who needed to be given the opportunity to grow. And, we as a team, throwing him in the front of everything else wasn't necessarily the best way to support this young kid who had just joined our team."

The rest of the world was doing that. From million-dollar endorsement deals to LeBron-centered merchandise everywhere to the most popular page on NBA.com, James certainly did not have to worry about lack of publicity.

"It wasn't going to be helped," continued Marek, "by us putting billboards of him up all over town or completely layering the market with television ads with his face all over them. I mean, he certainly was in an ad, but so were Darius [Miles] and Carlos [Boozer]."

The fact that LeBron possesses a "team-first" mentality made it a perfect plan to follow. Everybody was walking the same path.

"And I think if you look at the way the season unfolded," Marek said, "by the time it was over, that's what people were saying. And they weren't saying it because we were making them say it, they weren't saying it because we layered the market with things that said, 'We are a team.' They said it because they felt it."

GALA EVENT

The Cavaliers hosted a 2003 NBA Draft party at Gund Arena that attracted 10,000 people. The draft was broadcast on the Jumbotron.

"We had the number-one draft card there, LeBron's number 23 jersey, and the actual winning ping-pong ball," recalled

NBA commissioner David Stern shakes hands with LeBron James at the NBA Draft at Madison Square Garden on June 26, 2003. (Reuters/Landov)

Tracy Marek. "When our draft pick was made—which, of course, everyone in the world knew who it was going to be—we did a massive balloon drop, and it almost felt like Cleveland had just been chosen as the site for the next Olympics. It was that level of energy."

FIRST IMPRESSIONS FORGOTTEN FAST

Not long after the 2003 NBA Draft, the Cavaliers brought LeBron James to Gund Arena for a workout so he could meet Paul Silas, and to give the media a chance to talk to the young star. He was an hour late in showing up, which didn't sit too well with the 80-plus media members who were sweltering on the hot summer day.

"There we were," Rick Noland said, "standing around with tape recorders and cameras. You could already hear the grumbling: 'I'm 40 years old, I'm a grown man, and I'm at the beck and call of this 18-year-old kid.'

"And then he showed up. The workout basically consisted of him shooting about 20 free throws with Silas and then three-pointers from five different spots behind the arc while we all stood beyond half court and watched. I think he missed seven of the first 10 free throws, and the grumbling just kept getting worse: 'He can't shoot at all.' Then he went behind the three-point arc and he's just brickin' 'em away. The cynicism is just getting worse and worse."

Upon finishing his workout, James walked over to the media throng and turned on the ol' charm faster than any of them could hit record on their machines.

"And by the time he was done 15 or 20 minutes later," Noland continued, "he had captivated everybody in there. Everybody forgot he was an hour late getting there, everybody forgot how many free throws he had missed. I mean, he had everybody in the palm of his hand from that point on. He does that every time. Everyone thought he was going to be too cool, or egotistical, or this or that. But he's just a really nice kid. It's really hard to explain.

"The only guys I've ever seen able to do the same thing are Magic Johnson and Michael Jordan. They both have something about their personality that keeps you from disliking them or being jealous of their success."

KIDS CAN'T GET ENOUGH

It was apparent that LeBron James would be worshipped by youngsters right off the bat. Just take what happened in downtown Cleveland not long after the Cavaliers drafted him. LeBron was featured in a television commercial being filmed on Public Square.

"The kids were yelling and screaming at him," recalled Tracy Marek. "So it was really automatic, the energy he was bringing."

SUMMER SELLOUT
Gund Arena South

The NBA holds what it calls its Summer League in different venues nationwide. The league is made up of selected rookies and second-year players. When the LeBron James-led Cavaliers journeyed to Orlando for 2003 Summer League, they had no idea what was awaiting them. Normally, Summer League games draw 150 or so fans. When the Cavs pulled up to the

A future Cavalier sends happy wishes to LeBron James. (AP/WWP)

arena, they were in disbelief. All they saw was a throng of people around the building waiting to go in.

"I still can't believe it," said Tad Carper, who was along for the ride. "There were people out there actually scalping these tickets! And all the guys were just reacting, laughing like, 'I can't believe it!'"

When the hometown Magic took the floor, there was a polite, enthusiastic round of applause. But then when the Cavaliers—in practice jerseys, no less—came out, a thunderous roar cascaded from the stands. There were 20,000 people there—for a Summer League game!

"You would've thought we were inside Gund Arena," Carper recalled. "The place just erupted, and the guys were laughing in the lay up line. It was remarkable, especially after what we'd been through the last few years, to have that kind of reception. It wasn't uncommon, during the regular season when the Sixers or the Lakers or the Knicks came into Gund Arena, for the crowd to support them more than us. And to have the tables turned, to be in that environment down there against the home team and come out onto the floor, and the place just erupts, it gave you chills."

"And LeBron went out there right away," said Mike Snyder, "and did this reverse lay up, and the place went crazy."

For Darius Miles, Carlos Boozer and Dajuan Wagner, it must have felt like the twilight zone, considering what they had endured the year before.

"To be able to immediately bounce back," Carper said, "and be able to absorb that kind of environment, you could see the looks on their faces, how great it was for them to be a part of that."

What Is This, Rookie Hazing?

Before the game, LeBron's sense of humor surfaced. Once again, he shined in the spotlight—only with a different twist.

"He made sure," Carper recalled, "I think with egging on from Darius, that he was the last person in, and he walked into the building pulling one of our cargo trunks like that's rookie duty. I remember getting out of the car, walking in and seeing just a sea of media waiting for us, cameras, flashes going off, everything, and LeBron just coming in with a big smile on his face, pulling the cargo trunk, and Darius looking back over his shoulder yelling, 'C'mon, rook!'"

BOBBLEHEAD NIGHT
Springsteen? The Stones? No, Better

The lines started forming at 9 a.m. As morning turned to noontime, they grew. And as daytime turned to dinnertime, they grew...and grew...and grew. By 7 p.m., lines of people were wrapped around Gund Arena like a cat's tail wraps around its body while it's napping. The thousands of fans waiting to enter the building were such an awesome sight that had an outsider new to town walked by, they would have wondered, "What in the world is going on?"

What was going on was a Cleveland Cavaliers game against the Atlanta Hawks on this otherwise ordinary Wednesday evening in early March. Granted, rookie sensation LeBron James was leading the Cavs to a much-improved season over the year before. And, true, James is a hometown boy, hailing from nearby Akron. But this was a scene out of some never-never land. There had to be more to it than just a basketball game between two sub-.500 teams—even if King James *was* the stellar attraction.

There was.

The Cavaliers were running a promotion that night that was billed as "LeBron James Bobblehead Night." The first 10,000 fans through the gates were to receive a LeBron James Bobblehead Doll. The Gund was the place to be in Cleveland that night, and the chase was on to be one of the first 10,000 fans in line.

"It was an amazing sight to see," recalled Jeff Sack, "that amount of fans wrapped around Gund Arena. The only time I

Fans wait in line outside Gund Arena, hoping to get a LeBron James bobblehead doll on March 3, 2004. (AP/WWP)

had ever seen that was for concerts like Springsteen or when the Stones played there. And just to imagine that this edifice that had barely been able to attract 3,000 fans per game the season before had a line around the entire building like a rock concert was absolutely amazing."

Mike Snyder agreed but said it was even bigger than the Stones.

"I mean, I was down there for [The Rolling Stones]," he said, "and other concerts, and they didn't have anything like this."

Snyder knew it was going to be a big event—not this big, though.

"It was an amazing thing to see," he said.

Jim Paxson was in shock.

"I couldn't believe," he said, "when I'm looking out my office door and seeing people at 11 in the morning lined up on the walkway. I thought, 'This is unbelievable.'"

"By the time the gates opened," added Len Komoroski, "you probably had a good portion of the building waiting outside. And there was an aerial shot of everywhere around Gund Arena, lines just snaking around the entirety of the Gateway District waiting to get in line for their LeBron bobblehead."

Worth the Wait

Kenny Roda took the day off from work so he could take his son, Cameron, to the game. They went with a friend of Roda's and his son, too. The four of them had one goal in mind, and it was an obvious one: get a bobblehead.

"Since I was taking off work," Roda said, "I was going to make sure I was one of the first 10,000 down there. We probably got there about a quarter to five. It was like waiting at a turnstile at Cedar Point to go on one of the roller coasters. You just had to wait your turn, and nobody was upset with how long they had to wait—until all the bobbleheads were gone. Then, the people who didn't get them were upset that they didn't get there early enough.

"If you wanted one bad enough like I did, you would've done something like I did—take off work and make sure you're there early enough. We waited probably about 45 minutes to an hour, and that was no problem, no big deal. Even to my son, who was 12 at the time, it was no big deal to him because he was getting a LeBron James Bobblehead. He didn't complain once."

Bobbleheads and More Bobbleheads

Some fans were satisfied in receiving the LeBron James Bobblehead Doll they got the night of the giveaway. Some fans were not, though, and wanted more bobblehead dolls. Roda was one of them.

"A buddy of mine, Tom Culp," Roda said, "owns a sports store called Sportstown in North Royalton. We always talk about what's hot and what's not because he tries to get unique things at his store that people will want to buy.

"Well, I was down at the Cavs store early in the year and saw a three-and-a-half-foot LeBron bobblehead, and it was going for $450. I thought to myself, 'Do I want to spend $450 for this? I know it's unique, it's different, but do I want to spend it?' And I didn't."

Roda mentioned the super-sized bobblehead to Culp. He asked him if he could get one for him at cost. Culp told Roda he could not get him the exact same one but may be able to get a different version.

"So I said, 'Well, if they do, get me one,'" continued Roda, "'just get me one at cost, whatever it would cost.' So he called me back and said, 'It's in, it's a special, there are only 500 of them made. I got you number nine.' It's a three-and-a-half-foot LeBron bobblehead that's my fourth LeBron bobblehead, including my son's."

Wrong-Way Rush Hour

With Roda having taken the day off from his radio gig, Bob Karlovec filled in for him and hosted WKNR's *Happy Hour* show from Phil the Fire Restaurant. Karlovec recalled an amusing on-air exchange between himself and WKNR's traffic person.

"I kidded with her," he said, "about the fact that usually when she's talking about downtown traffic, it's getting *out* of the city in afternoon rush hour. But, that day, it was people trying to get *into* the city so they could get in line to get their LeBron bobblehead."

Bobblehead Blitzkrieg

LeBron James Bobblehead Night turned out to be, quite possibly, the most coveted giveaway in the history of professional sports. As the anticipation continued to build throughout the day and into the evening, the scene outside Gund Arena would have made for a fitting backdrop to the 1980s television show *That's Incredible*. It was a sight to behold.

It also left some 10,000 fans furious. Resonating loud and clear was the legendary "Law of Supply and Demand." Although the Cavaliers organization made it abundantly clear that only the first 10,000 fans would receive a bobblehead, it still didn't sit well with those left empty-handed.

"I thought it was brilliant," Bill Livingston said, "that they only had 10,000 bobbleheads."

Chad Estis found out firsthand just how frustrated those forsaken fans were. He was manning a table for season ticket holders for what the Cavaliers call "guaranteed giveaways." Season ticket holders can come to this table and receive one item from the giveaway that particular night. Thus, it was expected to be bustling at the "guaranteed giveaway" table on Bobblehead Night. What was not envisioned was an all-out assault.

"You can imagine," Estis said, "if you came in and you weren't one of the 10,000 who got one at the gate, and you're walking on the concourse and see a table with all these bobbleheads. You're thinking, 'How am I going to go over there and get one?'"

At one point, Estis was engulfed by 25-30 people interrogating him on how to obtain a bobblehead.

Fans watch postgame festivities with the LeBron James bobblehead doll in front of them after the game against the Hawks on LeBron James Bobblehead Night. (AP/WWP)

"There were questions like, 'What's this line for?'" he recalled, "and comments like, 'I'm a season ticket holder, but the account's not in my name.' We actually had a lot of people who shouldn't have been in line, or at the table, trying to get a bobblehead."

It became overwhelming. Believe it or not, Estis resorted to hopping onto a chair and shouting instructions on who should, and shouldn't be, in line. Season ticket holders secured a bobblehead upon presenting an ID card.

"When someone wants something like a bobblehead," Estis said, "they're coming up with any reason why they think they should get one. It never got to the point where it was out of control, but I just never anticipated, in my role, that I'd be standing on chairs screaming instructions at the crowd."

Gotta Have One

The LeBron James Bobblehead Doll was captivating the public. This seven and a half-inch caricature was sparking a swell of interest never seen before. Everybody under the sun, it seemed, wanted one—including LeBron's teammates.

"All the guys left with bobbleheads," Roda recalled, "so it wasn't just the fans. These are his own teammates, his peers, and these guys wanted bobbleheads of LeBron—signed!

"Paul Silas wanted one, too!"

Silas was bombarded with requests from those close to him.

"When people like that," Snyder said, "are having to get bobbleheads for friends or family, what does that say?"

Silas was not the only member of the Cavaliers organization to be besieged with requests for the doll. Paxson was, too.

"I'd get calls," he said, "like this: 'You know, all we really want is just a LeBron bobblehead. Are there any left?'"

There was even interest nationwide.

Said Len Komoroski, "We had people calling for tickets from California, and all over the nation, to see if they could get tickets to come to the game to be able to get a bobblehead."

"There were people waiting in line," added Roda, "who were going to send it to family or friends out of state who wanted one."

They're He-e-e-ere!

The Cavaliers organization went all out in planning the arrival of the LeBron James Bobblehead Dolls. A grand entrance amid enormous fanfare was the goal.

Objective achieved.

The first shipment of bobbleheads showed up courtesy of a Dunbar armored truck as a bit of a media stunt that was publicized big time.

"It came to our loading dock area," Komoroski recalled, "and we had our mascot, 'Moondog,' there to ride in on the passenger side. But then to sort of guide it in, he was 'one of the guards.' The media turnout was unbelievable, and the amount of national and international play that got was just staggering."

Bill Livingston compared the Cavs' PR ploy to stunts orchestrated by former Major League Baseball owner Bill Veeck, which included signing a midget to bat for the St. Louis Browns in 1951 and the infamous Disco Demolition Night during a White Sox/Tigers doubleheader in 1979.

"It got them on ESPN and all kinds of publicity around the country," Livingston said. "You have to give them that."

Bobblehead$ for $ale

Ebay's the way for many individuals selling items of interest. For some, that was the only reason they desired a LeBron James Bobblehead Doll. In fact, the doll was already on Ebay prior to the giveaway, fetching anywhere from $50-$300.

"There were even people denoting on it that they may not end up with one," Komoroski said, "but if they did, what it would cost."

"There were people waiting in line who were going to put it on Ebay," added Roda, "and others were going to try to get it signed and *then* put it on Ebay."

TAKE ONE! TAKE TWO!

After the Cavaliers' memorable upset of the Indiana Pacers on March 14 at Gund Arena, it was arranged for a young lady to conduct a mock television interview with LeBron James for a school project. LeBron was courteous and gracious, and even took a couple of pictures with her. After LeBron excused himself once the interview was finished, the fun began.

"Normally," Bob Karlovec recalled, "when they do the actual interview itself, they have the camera set up over the reporter's shoulder. So you're getting just the person who you're interviewing on camera. Then, after they leave, they'll bring the camera around, and they'll do shots of the person asking the questions.

"So, I remember they were doing shots of the girl asking the questions—again, so they could get a picture of her doing that so when they spliced the tape together, they could have a shot of her asking a question and then a shot of LeBron answering. And I remember that she would ask her question and then hold the mike up as if he was still there to get the answer. At one point, the guy who was doing the filming had to stop tape and roll up to her and say, 'You need to raise your hand higher.'"

Talk About a Road Trip!

There are road trips and then there are road trips. A family of four embarked on the mother of all road trips in the spring of LeBron's rookie season. These folks traveled all the way from Italy to see LeBron James play basketball. They ordered tickets off the Internet for the final two home games against Miami and Milwaukee.

"*The Plain Dealer* actually called and alerted us to this family," Len Komoroski said. "No one in the family spoke any English."

Because of the unique circumstances, the Cavaliers organization rolled out the red carpet. The family's original tickets, not the greatest seats in the world, were upgraded to much better ones.

"They even got a chance to do some extra special things," Komoroski continued. "They got a chance to go down on courtside on the bench during warmups, so they were able to actually meet LeBron. This family wasn't necessarily well off, either. They made the trip, but it wasn't as if they were independently wealthy."

Fishing for an Autograph

Some fans resorted to drastic measures to get an autograph from LeBron James. Perhaps the most creative attempt took place in Philadelphia. The Cavaliers were headed to practice for a shoot around. As the team walked underneath Wachovia Center, there was a throng of fans standing on a balcony some 15-20 feet above, screaming for autographs. There was no way they could reach the players from up there.

"Well, this one guy tied some kind of rope or string," recalled Ira Newble, "and lowered a shoe, and a pen with it, all the way down, dangling it so LeBron would run into it and sign it."

"I asked LeBron when he came in," Paul Silas said, "'Did you sign that thing?' He said, 'No, I didn't sign it.' I said, 'You should've because that was the most ingenious thing I've ever seen in my life.' It was unreal."

TALK THE TALK, WALK THE WALK

James professed one night after a game against Michael Redd and the Milwaukee Bucks that he and Redd were two of the premier players in the NBA. For a 19-year-old to publicly put himself in that class was bold, but also the truth.

"Not one reporter took exception to it," said Sack, "and if it had come from anybody else, I think they would've. But because it was LeBron, and he was able to walk the walk, as well as talk the talk, I think things like that were accepted."

I NEED MY REST

LeBron James became the first Cavalier ever to win the NBA Rookie of the Year award. It was really no surprise that he won the honor, but it was a shocker that he was 45 minutes late for the press conference in Cleveland. He overslept, thinking he had to go to practice that morning instead. Although a small

IN GOOD COMPANY

LeBron James in 2003-04 became just the third rookie in NBA history and first ever Cavalier to average 20-plus points, five-plus rebounds, and five-plus assists per game, averaging 20.9 points, 5.5 rebounds, and 5.9 assists. The two others to achieve the feat are Oscar Robertson in 1960-61 (30.5 ppg, 10.1 rpg, 9.7 apg) and Michael Jordan in 1984-85 (28.2, 6.5, 5.9).

contingent of the media members present were unforgiving, LeBron once again charmed his way out of the bad, and into the good, graces of most of them.

"Somebody asked him, 'What are you going to be spending your summer doing?'" Gordon Gund recalled. "And he said, 'Well, one thing I'm going to do is I'm going to relax and catch up on my sleep.' He had everybody there just in the palm of his hand in a very nice way. It was not contrived, but it just made you sense both the youth and the fact that he is only 19, and that's what a lot of 19-year-olds do. It was a wonderful moment."

"He's a kid, he's still a kid, he's 19," said Bob Karlovec. "And if he overslept, he overslept. From that standpoint, I'm going to cut him some slack. He still got there, we still had the press conference. Yeah, it would've been nice if he could've been there on time, but he was funny about it, he was apologetic about it."

"It certainly didn't bother we, the radio reporters, or the print reporters, too much," added Jeff Sack. "Some of the TV reporters were a little upset. I think, because he owned up to the fact that he was late, people were more accepting of it."

YES, IT'S ME, BUT I'M NOT HER
Wrong Number

When basketball fans in Northeast Ohio hear the name "Gloria James," a woman in her mid-30s comes to mind, a woman rightfully proud of her son's accomplishments, a woman who has been criticized for displaying her enthusiasm regarding LeBron's achievements.

When those same fans hear of "Gloria James," they don't think of a 66-year-old woman who lives on Cleveland's east side. Unfortunately for the elder Gloria James, fans frequently confused the two.

"After most every home game, win or lose, I'd get calls," said the second Gloria James. "The adults would just say, 'I'm sorry,' that they got my number off the computer. It got annoying at times, but it was rather humorous, too. I never really thought of changing my number. After the season, the calls stopped."

Mrs. James has had her phone number for several years. She received no calls whatsoever when LeBron was in high school.

"It didn't start happening until he got on the Cavaliers," she said. "No one ever came to the door, though."

Flower Power

Mrs. James was astonished when she received a bouquet of flowers from a gentleman in Tacoma, Washington. The man then telephoned her and said he had met her in Philadelphia.

"I've never been to Philadelphia in my life," she said, "and I had to explain that to him. When I told him I'm not LeBron's mother, he told me I could keep the flowers and that he was sorry. He said, 'It was nice talking to you.' But then he asked if he could call just to have prayers on the phone with me. He was really strange. I go to church, but nothing like that. So he began calling me periodically, and it was becoming a little odd."

Then, one day, Gloria's grandson, 26-year-old Jerome Wheeler, who lives there too, answered the phone, and on the other end of the line was the man who sent the flowers.

"Jerome was explaining to him it was the wrong number," Mrs. James said, "and the man asked my grandson, 'Well, what's your mother's name?' And he told him my daughter's name, and the man started to call her! I put a trace on the phone, and the authorities got involved. The calls stopped. That was about the closest I got to feeling I was in any danger."

Go to Your Room, Young Lady

When children would call Mrs. James, they would hang up for the most part. The teenage girls who phoned, however, would not. They would just giggle and profess their everlasting love for LeBron.

"Then they'd just get angry and cuss," she said, "when I'd tell them it was the wrong number. One of the girls got real nasty, so I got the number off the caller ID, and I called back. I explained to her grandmother what happened, and she told me, 'Oh no, I wouldn't have this.' So she told me when her daughter comes home, they'd call me back and put the girl on the phone.

"So the mother of the child called me back and said, 'Now, we're all going to speak to you, and you tell me what voice it was that talked to you.' So the grandmother said, 'Hello?' Then the girl said, 'Hello?' I said, 'That's the voice.' The girl kept on saying, 'It wasn't me, it wasn't me!' But it *was* her. The grandmother told me that I would never have this trouble again, and I didn't."

My Condolences

One time, the phone rang at 1:30 in the morning. Jerome answered, and it was a strange woman whose voice he did not recognize. He woke up his grandmother, and she got on the phone.

"She said, 'Gloria?'" Mrs. James recalled. "I said, 'Yes?' She said, 'I just wanted to let you know my grandson died.' And I said, 'But who are you?' And then she said she lived in Akron. I said, 'You know what? You got the wrong Gloria.' And she asked me, 'Well, isn't this LeBron's mother?' I said, 'No, it's not.'"

This Is Becoming Absurd

Mrs. James received a phone call one day from a young boy who said he was LeBron's brother.

"I said, 'No, LeBron doesn't have a brother,'" she recalled.

"I even so much as had a gospel group call one time to talk to LeBron."

Should I or Shouldn't I?

There were times when Jerome considered playing along with the phone calls. Then he came to his senses and used his better judgment.

"I thought about saying I was LeBron at times," he said, "but I decided, 'No, I'm not going to do that.'"

His grandmother should be proud of him.

Strange Looks

There were times when Gloria was out and about, and somebody would ask what her name was.

"I'd say, 'Gloria James,' she recalled. "They'd look at me, and I'd just tell them straight up and down, 'No, I'm not LeBron's mother. I wish I was.'"

MISSY'S GREAT ADVENTURE
Cool Concept

The Cavaliers organization staged numerous promotional giveaways throughout the 2003-04 season. And on Fan Appreciation Night for the home finale against the Milwaukee Bucks, they went all out. There were hundreds of giveaways that evening. Not one fan went home empty-handed.

The most anticipated giveaway was the one in which fans won Cavaliers game jerseys and shoes worn that night. The Cavaliers organization wanted to involve as many fans as possible. Thus, they split it up so one fan would receive a player's jersey, the next fan would get one of his shoes, and the next fan would get his other shoe. Then, it would be the same routine for the next player and the next three fans, and so on.

"It was designed," Tad Carper said, "to be a way for the players to really connect with the fans, to be sort of an outward reflection of the emotion that had generated internally over the course of the season."

"Just from personal experience," added Len Komoroski, "people are ecstatic because it's almost like not washing your hands. You've got the authentic sweat. ... I mean, that's authentic!"

"Most Exciting Moment of My Life"

Forty random ticket stub numbers were drawn during the game. The numbers appeared on screens high above midway through the third quarter. A 13-year-old girl by the name of Missy Arendash, from nearby Amherst, Ohio, was one of the lucky 40. It was Missy's first Cavaliers game of the season. The tickets were an Easter present from her parents, Ron and Sharon, to Missy and her younger sister, Jessie.

"I was crossing my fingers and hoping to get picked," Missy recalled. "My finger popped out because I was crossing it for so long. I flipped out when I saw my number up there. They said, as soon as you saw your number, you were supposed go down to the main level."

So Missy and her mother, who was actually holding her daughter's ticket, raced down there as fast as they could all the way from their nosebleed seats.

"They took my name and stuff," Missy continued, "and then I had to pick another number that told me what number I'd be to go out on the floor. I picked number 25, so I was 25th out of the 40 people. When I picked my number, the people who were running it said to me, 'Ooh, 25! That's a lucky number!' And I'm like, 'Okay.'"

Missy and the other 39 lucky souls were required to stand pat until the game was over.

"We got to watch the rest of the game from TV screens underneath," she said.

As soon as the game ended, Missy and the rest of the gang walked up to the floor and stood in line.

"They started giving the jerseys and shoes away," she recalled. "This lady came out with T-shirts and gave them to the players so they weren't standing there with no shirt on."

The 40 contestants had no idea which player they were going to be connected to.

"They didn't know what our system was," Tad Carper explained, "that the players were going to go numerically. And most of them, unless you're really studying the line and the system, you really didn't connect with it until you got right up there."

"There was this young girl," recalled Carper, "who you could see sort of counting and figuring out the system."

It was Missy.

Because the players lined up in numerical order, Jeff McInnis, who wears number 0, was first up. As Missy's turn was inching closer, the wheels in her head began to spin.

"If you figure it out," she said, "the 25th one is LeBron James's jersey, but I didn't figure that out until I was standing in line for awhile. So I had no idea what player's jersey or shoe I was going to get.

"I looked down and started counting the number of people ahead of me and how many jerseys and shoes were being given away. I'm thinking, 'Jersey, shoe, shoe, jersey, shoe, shoe,' and I figured out I was going to get a jersey. I was all excited, but I didn't know it was going to be LeBron's."

Missy thought she was going to receive Jason Kapono's number 24 jersey. Although she was disappointed it was not LeBron's, she was nonetheless tickled pink to get Kapono's jersey.

"I'm like, 'Cool, I'm getting Kapono,'" she said. "'I like him.'"

Missy was mistaken, though. She counted too far ahead.

"All of a sudden, the announcer goes, "Number 23, LeBro-o-o-on Ja-a-a-ames!" And I flipped out. I started crying and screaming. He came over and he's like, 'Here, kid.' I was freakin' out, looking up to him. I thought I was tall—I'm 5-11—this guy's like a giant, and I'm looking up to him and like, "H-h-h-hi-i-i-i, th-th-th-tha-a-a-anks. It was the most exciting moment of my life.

"I didn't get any sleep that night, either."

Call 911?

Missy was beside herself when she realized LeBron's jersey was hers. She was in shock. She almost missed out on all the fun that followed, too.

She nearly fainted.

"She started crying," Carper recalled. "She was screaming, she was shaking, I mean visibly shaking. And the crowd really reacted to it, too, when they saw her reaction to the realization that she was about to get handed LeBron James's game-worn jersey from that final home game of his first season by none other than LeBron James himself. She was just an emotional explosion happening right there at center court with him.

"At one point, I thought she might eventually need some help, that she really might faint or something. That was a very real thought in my mind at that time. I thought, 'My gosh, we're going to end up having to pick her up off the floor.'"

That's Not Fair!

According to the rules, none of the contest winners were to shake hands with the players. No autographs, no nothing. Although it might have been an arduous task for Missy to recover in time and get herself together enough to shake LeBron's hand, she said she could have.

"I watched the news later at home," she said, "and I saw the two guys behind me [who each got one of LeBron's shoes] shook his hand. I'm like, 'We weren't allowed to do that!' Trust me, I would've given him a hug or something!"

Who Needs College?

Missy has yet to wash LeBron's jersey. There is a purpose behind that.

"I have his DNA," she said. "I could clone him! Then I could be a zillionaire at 19, too."

Doctor's Orders

Missy had an appointment with her orthodontist the day of the Cavaliers season finale. She told him she was going to the game that night.

"He said, 'Well, you better bring garbage bags because they're giving out jerseys and shoes and everything,'" she recalled. "I was like, 'Oh yeah, right, like I'm going to get something like that.'"

NOW Do You Believe Me?

The next day at school, when Missy told her friends what happened to her the night before, they didn't believe her. They thought she just got a regular jersey.

"They're like, 'Oh, that's cool, I bought mine from Dick's Sporting Goods,'" she said. "I'm like, 'No guys, this is legit.'"

"It was about three weeks later, this kid comes in and says, 'Hey Missy, I saw you on TV. I'm like, 'For what?' And he's like, 'The LeBron jersey!' I'm like, 'Oh, that whole thing?' And the other kids are like, 'What LeBron jersey?' So I had to tell my whole study hall what happened. I was like, 'I told you!' And they're like, 'I want to see it now!'"

I Can Get a Cell Phone Anytime

One of the giveaways that evening was cell phones. Those are what fans in a section right next to the one the Arendashes were sitting in received.

"I'm like, 'Oh, no fair, I wanted a cell phone,'" Missy recalled. "They're all happy because they didn't just get a piece of paper saying they can go to a Sprint store, they passed out boxes of cell phones! I'm like, 'That's so-o-o-o sweet!' I was like, 'Man, I wish I won a cell phone.'

"But after winning what I did, thanks but no thanks to a cell phone."

Better Safe Than Sorry

A strange woman approached Missy as she and her mother were searching out her father and sister. Missy was holding the jersey she had won.

"The woman says, 'Dear, I'd put that on if I were you,'" Missy recalled. "'Someone could just snatch it and walk away.' So I'm like, 'Okay,' and I put it on.

"It's past my knees, and I'm 5-11!"

So This Is What It's Like to Be LeBron

As Missy and her family were leaving Gund Arena, several children spotted Missy and reacted as if she was a Hollywood star.

"They're all like, 'Oh my God, Mom, look, there's the girl!' and they're all freakin' out. I got an offer from some guy for $500. I said, 'No way, I know it's worth a lot more than that.' This girl comes up to me and says, 'Can I have my picture with you?' I'm like, 'Yeah, sure.' People were like, 'Can I touch it, can I touch it?'"

So, What Did YOU Do Over the Weekend?

In Missy's language arts class at school, they would go around the room, and the students would talk about how they spent the previous weekend. The Cavaliers game was on the

OPPONENTS ON LEBRON

" IT IS NOT HYPE ON LEBRON JAMES, THAT GUY CAN REALLY PLAY. THERE IS ONLY SO MUCH YOU CAN DO WITH A GUY WHO IS THAT BIG AND THAT TALENTED. HE DOES NOT LOOK LIKE A YOUNG GUY OUT THERE. HE PLAYS THE GAME WITH POISE. HE IS THE REAL DEAL AND WE ARE GOING TO BE DEALING WITH HIM FOR A LONG, LONG TIME. HE IS A HELL OF A PLAYER."

—*Stan Van Gundy*, Miami Heat head coach

Monday after Easter and was a vacation day for Missy's school district, making for a three-day weekend.

"I had the most exciting story of anyone," she said.

Maniacal Mom

Sharon Arendash was standing on the sidelines when her daughter won LeBron's jersey. Mrs. Arendash was quite possibly more excited than Missy herself.

"When I heard them announce it," she said, "I just went, 'Oh my God!'"

Sharon was the talk of the town the next day—at least on the Cavaliers' flagship radio station, WTAM-AM 1100. Mike Snyder, the floor announcer for the giveaway, was rehashing the events from the night before

"He said the girl who got it looked like she was going to pass out," Sharon recalled, "and that someone on the sidelines was jumping up and down screaming. ... I was jumping up and down screaming. I couldn't believe it. I was excited for her, I admit it. I was doing more screaming than her. She was in shock."

"They made fun of my mom," Missy added. "They said she was screaming so loud. They said she was a freak. She *was* a freak."

We're in the Money

The Arendash family recently took a vacation to Florida. They paid a visit to the NBA Store while down there and saw how much LeBron's jersey is worth.

"It was $1,000 I think, but it was autographed," Sharon said. "Even though ours isn't autographed, I don't think washing it would de-value it because I still have the letter saying this is the actual one [LeBron] wore that night. It's in a closet right now."

When James was named NBA Rookie of the Year, dollar signs flashed in the minds of the Arendashes.

"We were like, 'Oh my God!'" Sharon recalled. "A guy my husband works with said, 'I think your value just went up. Have the jersey and the Sharpie marker handy.' I can see it now, while other kids are handing LeBron programs and notepads for him to sign, Missy's handing him his own jersey."

Fun for All

Missy and her mother weren't the only ones on the Gund Arena floor who were enjoying themselves. LeBron wasn't having a bad time himself.

"He got a kick out of it, too," Carper said. "He had a big smile on his face. And that's the thing about LeBron; he was happy to see that it was a younger person who was getting it because he's really into connecting with kids."

Miss(y) America

Thirty minutes after she had been given LeBron's jersey, Missy was still emotional. She was in the concourse still in tears, and still in disbelief.

"It's almost like someone who won Miss America," Komoroski said, "when you have all the cameras around her when the crown is put on her head. You literally had about 15 television cameras around her, and photographers, capturing that moment. Her hands were shaking and trembling and just the tears flowing out of her face…it was spectacular. It was everything you could hope for."

A Hollywood Ending

Missy's big night was a fitting finale to the fun-filled rookie season of LeBron James. It could not have been scripted any better.

"It was just one of those little moments," Carper said, "where the kids—young kids and teenagers alike in the community—just really had a connection with LeBron, and still do for that matter. It was almost as if this young girl was representing the emotions of so many kids her age, to be down there on the floor accepting that from just a small little point of connection and thank you from [LeBron] to the fans for the season. There she is, holding on to his sweaty jersey."